T0113889

ANCHORED

RESILIENT FAITH

+

RELENTLESS OBEDIENCE

TURHONDA S. FREEMAN

WESTBOW
PRESS®
A DIVISION OF THOMAS NELSON
& ZONDERVAN

This book is a work of non-fiction. Unless otherwise noted, the author and the publisher make no explicit guarantees as to the accuracy of the information contained in this book and in some cases, names of people and places have been altered to protect their privacy.

WestBow Press books may be ordered through booksellers or by contacting:

WestBow Press
A Division of Thomas Nelson & Zondervan
1663 Liberty Drive
Bloomington, IN 47403
www.westbowpress.com
844-714-3454

Because of the dynamic nature of the Internet, any web addresses or links contained in this book may have changed since publication and may no longer be valid. The views expressed in this work are solely those of the author and do not necessarily reflect the views of the publisher, and the publisher hereby disclaims any responsibility for them.

Unless marked otherwise, all Scripture quotations are taken from the New King James Version®. Copyright © 1982 by Thomas Nelson. Used by permission. All rights reserved.

Scripture quotations marked AMP are taken from the Amplified® Bible, Copyright © 2015 by The Lockman Foundation. Used by permission.

ISBN: 978-1-6642-8084-7 (sc)
ISBN: 978-1-6642-8083-0 (e)

Library of Congress Control Number: 2022918958

Print information available on the last page.

WestBow Press rev. date: 12/17/2022

Oh, hello there! I'm so glad you're here. We are getting ready to embark upon a wonderful and rewarding journey of studying God's Word together and I can hardly contain my excitement.

It's an absolute honor meeting you in the pages of a familiar story that has been told countless times. It was nearly 3 years ago when I started studying Noah with curiosity and intentionality. Of course, probably like you, I've heard the story of the Flood, the Ark and the Rainbow more times than I can remember. It's one of those bible stories that we learn as children. If you're like me, you can recite Noah's narrative like a well-rehearsed Easter speech. But I specifically remember one day reading Genesis 6 when a light flickered inside my heart. As I began to dig deeper, I found treasures of revelation that made me want to leap. So, here I am, leaping into this bible study - - my heart wide open with the expectation that you'll leap along with me.

Over the next 6 weeks, we will use the S-E-E-D Bible Study Method to guide us. Whether you have 20 minutes or 2 hours, this tool is intended to simplify and enhance your study time while promoting a habit of daily-digging. At the end of each day's devotion, the S-E-E-D verse is provided to invite you into a more in-depth study. I encourage you to use those verses to dig as much or as little as you desire. To get you started, we will spend the 1st week learning how to use and apply the S-E-E-D Bible Study Method.

It is my prayer that you will see yourself in Noah's story and that God will give you a fresh perspective on what it means to be "Anchored." My prayer is also that you'll dig deep into God's Word with the same curiosity and fervor that compelled me to write. I am confident that God is going to meet us here. Are you ready?

Let's dig…

TuRhonda S. Freeman

CONTENTS

WEEK 4: WAIT

WEEK 5: THE ANCHOR

WEEK 6: WORSHIP

WEEK 1

THE PREPARATION

DAY 1

"THE S-E-E-D BIBLE STUDY METHOD"

The Bible is not some complicated book of ancient words and hidden codes. It is the very Word of God given to us as a roadmap to navigating the Christian journey. Some call it old, outdated and irrelevant. But we call it alive, active and the answer to every question of this culture.

> *For the word of God is living and active and full of power [making it operative, energizing, and effective]. It is sharper than any two-edged sword, penetrating as far as the division of the soul and spirit [the completeness of a person], and of both joints and marrow [the deepest parts of our nature], exposing and judging the very thoughts and intentions of the heart.* ~ Hebrews 4:12 AMP

Why is studying the Bible so important? There are many reasons. The most compelling one is that the Bible is the only book that with many human writers but one

Divine Author - - God Himself. The Bible is described as being "God-breathed". In 2 Timothy 3:16, Paul reminds us that *'all Scripture is given by inspiration of God, and is profitable for doctrine, for reproof, for correcting, for instruction in righteousness.'*

HOW TO STUDY THE BIBLE?

Read it carefully and prayerfully.
Ask questions.
Pay close attention to the context.
Read it with a readiness to obey.

The S-E-E-D Bible Study method was created as a tool to simplify and deepen your study time. Whether you have 20 minutes or 2 hours to S-E-E-D, you can expect to walk away with a personal revelation every single time. The more you dig into God's Word, the more treasure you'll uncover. And that is what makes studying the Bible so powerful.

HOW TO USE THE S-E-E-D BIBLE STUDY METHOD:

S - Scripture

Select one Scripture or passage of Scripture to focus on. Read it at least 2-3 times. Then, write it down in a notebook/journal word-for-word. Then read it once again (preferably out loud), taking your time to allow each word to soak into your thoughts.

E - Examine

Context is everything. Dig deeper into the Scripture to understand its overall meaning. Read the verses before and after it, preferably the entire chapter, making note of the "big picture." Read it in another translation. Find 1-2 cross-reference verses that support the main point that the writer is making. Look up the definition of a word from the verse. Read the notes from a study bible or a bible commentary.

Use reliable sources such as www.BlueLetterBible.org, a Bible Dictionary and/or Lexicon to examine the scripture in greater depth.

Write down any facts that you've learned about your reading to help you gain deeper insight (perhaps using the Five W's — Who, What, When, Where and Why).

E - Envision

What do you see in this verse?
How does it speak to you?
What is your takeaway from the scripture?
Think about ways to apply this scripture to your personal life or situation.

D - Declare

Turn your thoughts to prayer.
Write out a prayer of declaration.
Thank God for planting this scripture in your heart.

DAY 2

"S = SCRIPTURE"

Picture this…

You are a gardener that has been given **one seed** to plant, water and grow. Think about your level of expertise, past and present experiences and overall perspective on seeds. This one that you have been given is special. As a gardener, you'll want to nurture it with precision and grace. You'll want to understand its anatomy, background, and maturation. You'll want to watch over your seed to make sure it becomes all that the Creator intended for it to be.

Today, you have the unique opportunity to handpick your seed.

Choose a verse of scripture that will guide your study time for the first week. This is your seed. It could be one that is familiar, one that has been nagging at your spirit, one that you want to know more about, or one that challenges, puzzles or inspires you in this season of life.

Write your S-E-E-D verse below…

_____

_____

_____

Once you've chosen your scripture, read it several times to yourself. At this point, you are not trying to interpret each word of the scripture, but you are starting to commit it to memory. Read prayerfully and purposefully.

Then, write the scripture in a notebook or journal word for word.

Finally, read the scripture again - - this time reading it out loud. Pause over words that you need to reflect more on. Allow each word of the scripture to soak into your thoughts.

The beautiful dichotomy in choosing _one seed_ from the Word of God is that you can't plant just one. The very purpose of a seed is to germinate and bring forth life. Once you start digging into the Word, you'll see the evidence of roots, which will lead to even more digging. As a result of consistency, harvest will come. And you, my friend, will never be the same.

DAY 3

"E = EXAMINE"

Write your S-E-E-D verse below...

_____

_____

_____

Are you ready to roll up your sleeves and get your hands dirty with S-E-E-D?

Examining the text is the most critical component of understanding how to apply it to your personal life. So, take your time during this phase of the process. This is where you will put on the hat of an experienced cross-examiner - - asking questions, looking for clues, connecting the dots.

Before applying any truth from Scripture, you must first understand its meaning. Why? Because context is everything. Understanding how your chosen verse relates to the verses around it is important. So, read your verse again. Then, read the verses before and after it. Sometimes you may need to read the entire chapter and/or the entire book in order to understand the "big picture" the author wants to convey. As you read, see if you can answer these questions:

Who?
What?
When?
Where?
Why?

To help guide your digging, use a reliable resource such as a Bible Dictionary and/or Lexicon to examine the scripture in greater depth. A study Bible can also be helpful in providing historical/cultural information on the text, pointing out cross-reference scriptures that relate to your chosen verse, and giving thorough theological explanations. Most Bibles provide a historical overview or introduction at the beginning of the book. BlueLetterBible.org is a free online resource that offers a concordance, dictionary, text commentaries and cross-references all in one place.

A simple approach is to use an English dictionary to define one or two words from your chosen verse. Even if you know what a word means, sometimes there are other definitions that may add more context. Then, use a bible dictionary to understand what the word meant in the original language that it was written. As you dig, write down any facts or clues that you find.

It is important to use the resources mentioned, but don't rely on them to do all the work for you. Examine the text for yourself. Follow the trails of treasure, making a note of every gem that you discover. As you study, ask the Holy Spirit to help you interpret what you are reading.

DAY 4

"E = ENVISION"

Write your S-E-E-D verse below...

_____

_____

_____

The hardest part about envisioning the text is allowing God to illuminate it. It can be tempting to take a verse out of context because we agree or disagree with what it says on the surface. As believers, we don't force the Scripture to fit our circumstances. Instead, we accept the interpretation (its _meaning and intention_) of the Scripture as God's Holy Word.

The first recorded words of God are found in Genesis 1:3, 'Then God said, "_Let there be light"; and there was light_'. God's Word is not only a lamp under our feet, but a light on our path (Psalm 119:105). Light shines, illuminates, reveals, clarifies, teaches and enhances. It is by the light of the Word that we are able to see our way.

Today, as a result of digging, you should have a better understanding of your S-E-E-D verse. Look back over the evidence that you collected as you examined the text.

As you stand in the light of revelation, the question is: what do you see in your chosen verse?

How does it speak to you?
What is your takeaway from the scripture?
In what ways can you apply this scripture to your personal life or situation?

When context gets cloudy, when your understanding is challenged and stretched, when darkness looms, pray this: 'Lord, let there be light.' Then, trust the light that the Holy Spirit provides.

So, again, what do you see? Write your observations below…

_____

_____

_____

DAY 5

"D = DECLARE"

Write your S-E-E-D verse below…

_____

_____

_____

Today, you will turn your thoughts into a prayer of declaration. Look back over all that you've learned about your selected verse. Think about the revelation that has come as a result of your digging. Now, let's pray and declare God's Word over your life.

Making a declaration is an important part of the process. It is how the Word begins to take root in our hearts. The words we speak are a direct result of what we believe to be true. Your prayer of declaration is based on a truth that you have discovered for yourself. Make no mistake, though. Declaring the Word is not a magic formula to use as you see fit. Powerful change only happens when our resilient faith and relentless obedience align succinctly with God's perfect and divine will.

Today, with a heart that has been pricked by revelation and postured in obedience, make a prayer of declaration using your S-E-E-D verse.

_____

_____

_____

WEEK 2

THE ASSIGNMENT

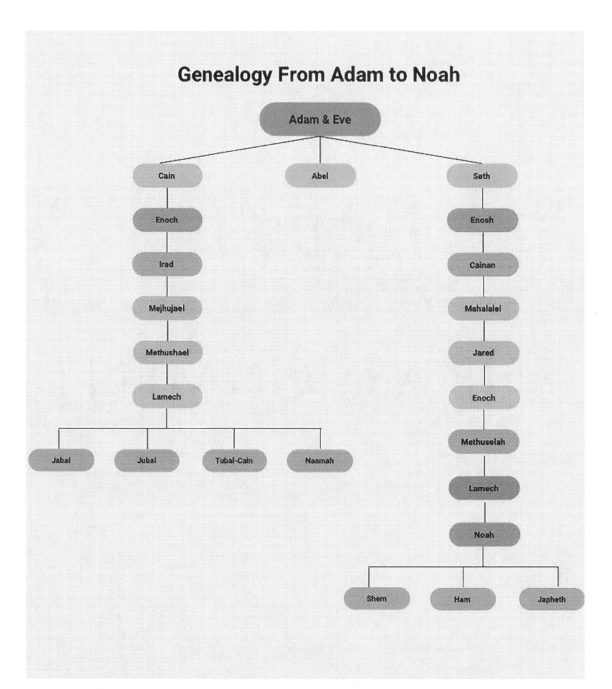

Adam to Noah – 10 Generations of families on earth pre-Flood

DAY 1

"IN THE BEGINNING"

Genesis 6:9 ~ These are the generations of Noah. Noah was a righteous man, blameless in his generation. Noah walked with God.

Noah's story is one of obedience, redemption and restoration. It has been told countless times in countless ways. Noah was the tenth generation descendent of Adam, the first human being on earth. The genealogy connects Adam to Noah's family, who survived the Flood and became the first in God's re-creation story. Noah's father was Lamech, but his mother's name is unknown. His grandfather was Methuselah, the oldest person in the Bible, who died in the year of the Flood at the age of 969.

The pre-Flood conditions of God's earth contributed to its unusually long life. You can liken it to a literal heaven on earth. When we look at the history of creation in Genesis 1, the Bible indicates that God made the firmament and divided it into 2 bodies of water - - the one above He called Heaven and the one below He called Earth. (Genesis 1:6-10) Merriam Webster's dictionary[1] defines **firmament** as the vault or arch of the sky; heavens. John MacArthur's Study Bible[2] notes that the *waters under the firmament were the subterranean (or underground) reservoirs. The waters above the firmament could have been a canopy of water vapor that made the earth like a hothouse, provided uniform temperature, inhibited mass air movements, caused a mist to fall, and filtered out ultraviolet rays, thus extending life.* Because of God's flawless creation of Heaven and Earth, there was never a need for rain - - that is, until God needed to hit the reset button. He used Noah (*whose Hebrew name means "rest" and "comfort"*) to draw a great dividing line in world history.

During Creation, God placed windows in the Heavens, which would later be the portals wherein rain could water the earth. (Genesis 7:11) You should take notice of God's brilliance and perfection in creation. When He divided the waters, He stood on the edge of the universe - - peeking through space and time - - to see a need for rain at some point in eternity. When the appointed time would come for the earth to need rain, He had already made provision for it. Notice that God never created anything else after His rest on the 7th day. It was finished.

Job had the audacity to petition God to court to prove his innocence. When God responded, His face-to-face interrogation of Job left him speechless.

Job 38:4-11 "Where were you when I laid the foundation of the earth? Tell me, if you have understanding. ⁵ *Who determined its measurements— surely you know! Or who stretched the line upon it?* ⁶ *On what were its bases sunk, or who laid its cornerstone,* ⁷ *when the morning stars sang together and all the sons of God shouted for joy?* ⁸ *"Or who shut in the sea with doors when it burst out from the womb,*

This is a time of rejoicing. Why? Because the same God who fashioned the universe with His words is the **same God** who knew you before the foundations of the world. Take a look at Ephesians 1:4 and record the keywords that the Apostle Paul uses to describe this truth: (fill in the blank)

Just as He _____ in Him _____ of the world, that we should be _____ and _____ before Him _____ ...

> [9] when I made clouds its garment and thick darkness its swaddling band, [10] and prescribed limits for it and set bars and doors, [11] and said, 'Thus far shall you come, and no farther, and here shall your proud waves be stayed'?
>
> Check out the full passages in Job 38-39.

This verse (Ephesians 1:4) speaks to the doctrine of election, which emphasizes that God not only chose us (as believers) *by Himself,* but also *for Himself* to the praise of His own glory. So, right at the start of this bible study, settle in your spirit that you are chosen. You are exactly where you should be at this moment in time. The fact that we are meeting in the pages of this study is no coincidence. You were *chosen* to be here.

Write the words to the verses below. Then, circle the action words that describe God's involvement in choosing His creation.

Psalm 139:13 _____

Jeremiah 1:5 _____

DIG DEEPER

Isaiah 44:24

Thus says the LORD, your Redeemer, and He who formed you from the womb: I am the Lord, who makes all things, who stretches out the heavens all alone, who spreads abroad the earth by Myself.

S – SCRIPTURE

_____

_____

_____

E – EXAMINE

_____

_____

_____

E – ENVISION

_____

_____

_____

D – DECLARE

_____

_____

_____

DAY 2

"THE DAY SIN GAVE BIRTH"

Genesis 6:1-5

Now it came to pass, when men began to multiply on the face of the earth, and daughters were born to them, ² that the sons of God saw the daughters of men, that they *were* beautiful; and they took wives for themselves of all whom they chose.

³ And the Lord said, "My Spirit shall not strive with man forever, for he *is* indeed flesh; yet his days shall be one hundred and twenty years." ⁴ There were giants on the earth in those days, and also afterward, when the sons of God came in to the daughters of men and they bore *children* to them. Those *were* the mighty men who *were* of old, men of renown.

⁵ Then the Lord saw that the wickedness of man *was* great in the earth, and *that* every intent of the thoughts of his heart *was* only evil continually.

In Genesis 6, we are getting a birds-eye-view of a wicked and perverted culture. It was an era in which sin, corruption, sensuality, hatred, violence and evil spread like wildfire. The sin nature of man had completely consumed and corrupted them from the inside out. Mankind was so puffed up with their own selfish power that the 'sons of God' married the 'daughters of men', giving birth to a wicked race of rebellious offspring, thus repeating the endless cycle of extreme iniquity. Let's draw a parallel between Genesis 6:1-5 and James' warning to the Church.

Write the words from James 1:14-15 _____

According to James 1, there is a process between sin's conception and its birth. It is likened to the same process of physical conception and birth. When a woman conceives, she undergoes a series of supernatural changes in her physical body. When the baby that she is carrying comes to full maturity, then she can give birth. James describes sin in a four-step process:

Desire → deception → disobedience → death

Desire (or temptation) is the seed of sin - - which is lying dormant in our own hearts. It is part of our spiritual makeup. Notice how the scripture says '*he is drawn away by his own desires*' (verse 14). It is a very personal, intimate seed inside each of us. And it does not play fair. Sin will not negotiate with you - - its seed has a strong, stubborn desire to rule your life. Fight back. Starve the seed of temptation. Deny it the breath and vitality it needs to grow.

Deception is the second stage of sin. It involves the lies that we believe and accept as truth. "Enticed" describes the deception that believers fall into - - one that captures our attention, traps our thoughts, and overshadows our best intentions to do good. Deception is the part of sin that is pleasing to our individual nature - - and it can be different for each person based on upbringing, inherited tendencies, personal experiences, etc.

What does James say plainly in verse 16? _____

Disobedience is the third stage of sin. It is the personal choice that begins in our minds and makes its way to our actions. What started as a seed has now matured into blatant disobedience, leading to sin's fourth and final stage. James 1:15b - *and sin, when it is full-grown, brings forth death.* The inevitable result of sin is always death. It is God's judgment on the disobedience of mankind, which was introduced by the first man, Adam. For all of eternity, Adam will be the first man who collapsed under the weight of disobedience, resulting in the universal experience of physical death.

In Romans 5:12-21, Paul draws a line of comparison between death in Adam and life in Christ.

What are your observations and thoughts from these verses? _____

Paul describes four 'reigns' in the passage. What are they?

_____

In your opinion, how does the world's attitude toward sin today compare with its attitude toward sin in Noah's day? _____

DIG DEEPER

1 Corinthians 10:13

No temptation has overtaken you except such as is common to man; but God *is* faithful, who will not allow you to be tempted beyond what you are able, but with the temptation will also make the way of escape, that you may be able to bear *it*.

S – SCRIPTURE

_____

_____

_____

E – EXAMINE

_____

_____

_____

E – ENVISION

_____

_____

_____

D – DECLARE

_____

_____

_____

DAY 3

"AND GOD GRIEVED"

Genesis 6:5-7

"Then the Lord saw that the wickedness of man *was* great in the earth, and *that* every intent of the thoughts of his heart *was* only evil continually.

And the Lord was sorry that He had made man on the earth, and He was grieved in His heart.

So the Lord said, "I will destroy man whom I have created from the face of the earth, both man and beast, creeping thing and birds of the air, for I am sorry that I have made them."

Have you ever stopped for a moment to consider what kind of actions would grieve our Lord? Genesis 6 describes a wickedness that is seemingly distant - - one that we can barely comprehend and feel selfishly far removed from. Man, whom God created from the dust of the ground, had become increasingly wicked. Verse 5 indicates that *every intent of the thoughts of his heart was only evil continually.* This is a loaded statement. It means that there was not one single aspect of man's nature that had not been corrupted by sin. Not one. It also indicates that there was a deep level of immoral decay at the very core of man's being. As a result, God was sorry and grieved. The word *grieved* describes a deep sorrow - - not because God lacked control or was caught off guard by mankind's actions - - but, in the face of human sin and rotten rebellion, He *felt* sorrow. This word – sorrow – is what Bible scholars call *anthropopathic*[3] which characterizes God as having human feelings and emotions. But don't you dare reduce our Holy God to the same fickle and fleeting emotions that we possess. He is unchangeable and has emotions that reflect the true nature of His character: just, true and perfect (Deuteronomy 32:4).

Nevertheless, we do not serve a God who is out-of-touch, unaffected, or detached. Aren't you glad about that? Not only is He aware of our feelings, He is well-acquainted with them. Hebrews 4:15 is a perfect picture of the genuineness of Christ's humanity – *"For we do not have a High Priest who cannot sympathize with our weaknesses, but was in all points tempted as we are, yet without sin."*

Below are some emotional characteristics that the Bible attributes to God:

love (John 3:16, Romans 5:8)
hate (Psalm 5:5)
compassion (Exodus 33:19)
grief (Genesis 6:6)
joy (Nehemiah 8:10)
rejoicing (Isaiah 65:19)
jealousy (Joshua 24:19)

When it was clear that God's plans for humanity were being trampled upon by sin, He found one man with whom He could begin again. History would remember him as Noah.

Which one of God's emotional characteristics can you identify with during this season of your life? _____

What other truths does Hebrews 4:14-16 point out about our Great High Priest?

_____

_____

DIG DEEPER

Zephaniah 3:17
The Lord your God in your midst,
The Mighty One, will save;
He will rejoice over you with gladness,
He will quiet *you* with His love,
He will rejoice over you with singing."

S – SCRIPTURE

_____

_____

_____

E – EXAMINE

_____

_____

_____

E – ENVISION

_____

_____

_____

D – DECLARE

_____

_____

_____

DAY 4

"RELENTLESS GRACE"

Genesis 6:8 "But Noah found grace in the eyes of the Lord."

Let's take a flashback glance at God's judgment on humanity because of the widespread wickedness. Genesis 6:3: And the LORD said, *"My Spirit shall not strive with man forever, for he is indeed flesh; yet his days shall be one hundred and twenty years."* This statement can be likened to a grace period being extended to an undeserving people. There was 120 years between God deciding to destroy mankind and the Flood occurring. Make note that we don't have to wait until Christ our Savior is revealed on the earth to see the grace of God. Throughout the pages of scripture - - from Genesis to Revelation - - grace is alive and well. Grace was in the Garden of Eden when Adam and Eve transgressed against God. And every generation thereafter has been direct beneficiaries of God's relentless grace.

Why do you think Genesis 6:8 indicates that Noah "found" grace?

_____

Grace was certainly not lost. It is quite possible that Noah found grace because he was actively looking for it. Perhaps Noah was moved by the knowledge that sin would be pregnant for 120 years and it was destined to bring forth death. Perhaps Noah went searching for answers and direction amid the ungodliness. Perhaps Noah went seeking a way to escape the inevitable destruction. Whatever his reason, the scriptures are clear that Noah *found* grace.

What does the second half of Romans 5:20 promise?

_____

Noah found a grace that would forever etch his name in history. This was not an ordinary grace - - like the grace you speak over your food at breakfast. It was a ground-breaking, earth-shattering, life-saving, undeserving grace. The end of mankind was approaching, and instead of piles of destruction, Noah found grace piled upon grace. (John 1:16)

In what ways have you experienced God's relentless grace in your life?

_____

DIG DEEPER

Romans 5:5
Now hope does not disappoint, because the love of God has been poured out in our hearts by the Holy Spirit who was given to us.

S – SCRIPTURE

_____

_____

_____

E – EXAMINE

_____

_____

_____

E – ENVISION

_____

_____

_____

D – DECLARE

_____

_____

_____

DAY 5

"THE ASSIGNMENT OF A LIFETIME"

Noah accepted a life-altering assignment that left lasting effects on the entire world. It was not an assignment that he'd signed up for - - but one that God hand-picked him to carry out. Dictionary.com[4] defines an assignment as a position or post of duty to which one is assigned. The assignment was bigger than Noah could have imagined. It was complex. It was larger-than-life. It was messy at times. And yet, Noah responded in complete obedience.

Let's pause right here.

There was only one possible, sane way Noah could carry out the divine assignment on his life: by grace.

> **2 Corinthians 9:8 ~ And God *is* able to make all grace abound toward you, that you, always having all sufficiency in all *things*, may have an abundance for every good work.**

Like Noah, you have been called-out and set-apart by God with a divine assignment tailor-made for you. It is an assignment that only you can do. Someone else may have the same talents and skills, but they cannot carry out what God has assigned specifically to you.

You might agree that it's easy to accept an assignment that you are well-prepared for. But what about the assignments that you don't ask for? What about the assignments that stretch you far beyond your level of comfort? What about the assignments that leave you with more questions than answers?

Noah didn't ask to be favored, but he was. The grace of God is extended to us in ways that we cannot always fathom - - preparing and equipping us to carry out every assignment, both big and small.

Just for a moment, think about "the assignment" that you are on right now. Make no mistake about it. You are on assignment. And how you handle the assignment is critical to your destiny.

Whether it is your job, family, children, your circle of friends, or at your church, or in your community, or in your hometown…you are on assignment.

Repeat it out loud: "I AM ON ASSIGNMENT"

In 1 Kings 17-18, God took Elijah through a series of assignments to prepare him for the assignment of a lifetime on Mount Carmel. God used the assignments to train Elijah in the art of faith and obedience. God made provisions for him - - causing water to flow from the brook and sending ravens to feed him there. Elijah did not have to look for provision. It was waiting on him. Then, when it was time to get up and move on to the next assignment, the brook dried up.

In your own words, why do you think the brook dried up?

_____

What was the significance of Elijah's assignment with the widow (1 Kings 17:8-16)?

_____

Today, think about these statements as you discover and live out your God-appointed assignment:

In Mike Murdock's book "The Assignment[5]," he identifies 31 facts to understand your assignment. Here are 5 of them:

Let's take a "Selfie Assessment." To fulfill any God-ordained assignment, you need His anointing and grace. What task or assignment have you taken on (either now or in the past) that caused you to do it in your own strength? What did you learn about yourself as a result?

1. EVERYTHING GOD CREATED WAS CREATED TO SOLVE A PROBLEM (Jeremiah 1:7, 8; I Corinthians 7:20; Genesis 2:18, 21 – 23; Psalm 127:3; 128:3, 4; Revelations 4:11)
2. YOUR ASSIGNMENT WILL ACQUIRE YOUR TOTAL FOCUS (Deuteronomy 13:6 – 10; Matthew 5:29 – 30; Matthew 6:33)
3. YOUR ASSIGNMENT WILL REQUIRE SEASONS OF PREPARATION (Acts 7:22, 23 – 31; Galatians 4:4-5; Acts 23:6; Job 23:10)
4. YOUR ASSIGNMENT IS GEOGRAPHICAL (John 4:4)
5. NEVER STAY WHERE YOU HAVE NOT BEEN ASSIGNED (Matthew 10:14)

Let's Pray:

Father, I thank You for the assignment I am on right now. I embrace it fully. Train me in the skill of faith and obedience. Teach me how to carry out my assignment with both grace and grit.

DIG DEEPER

Isaiah 1:19

If you are willing and obedient,
You shall eat the good of the land;

S – SCRIPTURE

_____

_____

_____

E – EXAMINE

_____

_____

_____

E – ENVISION

_____

_____

_____

D – DECLARE

_____

_____

_____

WEEK 3

WORK

DAY 1

"THE HIGHLIGHT REEL"

Genesis 6:9-10

This is the genealogy of Noah. Noah was a just man, perfect in his generations. Noah walked with God. And Noah begot three sons: Shem, Ham, and Japheth.

To understand why God chose Noah, let's unpack the characteristics that are used to describe him. Notice that verse 9 states that *this is the genealogy of Noah* - - which is an account of the ancestry or lineage of an individual or group of people. Sandwiched between Noah's genealogy is the highlight reel of his character.

Noah was:

A just man – Some Bible translations use the word *'righteous.'* This means that Noah was an innocent man in right standing and right relationship with God. Other words used to describe 'a just man' are upright, honest, virtuous and pious. Considering the cesspool of sin and wickedness during Noah's day, he lived a life that was unaffected by his surroundings.

In your own words, how was Noah able to maintain his righteousness despite the society that he lived in? _____

How did Peter describe Noah in 2 Peter 2:5? _____

Perfect in his generations - signifying that time and history would remember a man whose genetic integrity stood out amongst the rest of the culture. Simply put, Noah was good in the very core of his being.

The word 'perfect' in this verse comes from the root word *tāmîm*, meaning without blemish or spot, whole, complete, unimpaired, innocent and having integrity[6].

Psalm 19:7-9 gives a revelation of the purity and perfection of the word of God. Write down each of the 6 truths found in these verses and their corresponding effect.

This is the Truth	**This is the Consequence of the Truth**
1. The law of the LORD is perfect	1. It converts the soul
2.	2.
3.	3.
4.	4.
5.	5.
6.	6.

The value of the scriptures cannot be compared with any other desirable or worthy thing - - not even the purest form of gold. Verse 10 goes on to say that "more to be desired are they than gold, yea, than much fine gold."

Noah's character being likened to 'perfect' is no lightweight accomplishment. It was major, especially considering every thinkable influence to go astray. Noah stood the test of time.

Walked with God – a continual pattern of life, marking a contrast between Noah and the rest of the people of his day.

In our culture, a highlight reel is a snapshot of the best moments of someone's life. There is a gravitational pull toward things that either look great on camera, or can be captured in a 30-second reel, or be summed up in 280 characters on Twitter.

The highlight reel of Noah's character was not that he was a perfect man - - it was that he walked *with* God when everyone else walked *away from* Him.

What does the highlight reel of your life reveal about your character?

_____

DIG DEEPER

Colossians 3:3

For you died, and your life is hidden with Christ in God.

S – SCRIPTURE

_____

_____

_____

E – EXAMINE

_____

_____

_____

E – ENVISION

_____

_____

_____

D – DECLARE

_____

_____

_____

DAY 2

"WALKING WITH REVELATION"

The scriptures record that Noah walked with God. This points to a level of intimacy (familiarity, closeness, and affection) unknown to any other person at the time. While everyone else turned their backs on God, walked away from Him, did whatever was pleasing in their own eyesight, perpetuated evil and iniquity...Noah walked with God.

You must determine in your heart that when everyone else is turning away from God, chasing after their own passions and lusts, manipulating their own results … you are the one who will remain.

Let's look at Jesus's description of what it means to *remain*.

> **John 15:5-6** ~ "I am the vine, you are the branches. He who abides in Me, and I in him, bears much fruit; for without Me you can do nothing. If anyone does not abide in Me, he is cast out as a branch and

is withered; and they gather them and throw them into the fire, and they are burned."

The word "abide" means to remain, to dwell, to settle in, to stay around, to sink deeper[7].

The benefits of abiding are highlighted in verse 7:

If you _____ in Me, and My words
_____ in you, you will ask what you desire, and
it _____ .

When everyone else is … self-promoting, self-loathing, self-serving … you are the one who will remain, dwell, settle in, stay around and sink deeper into the Lord.

Noah abided with God. He was "the one" who had been hand-picked by God. Being "the one" is not for the faint at heart: you may feel isolated and left out. But, are you willing to take isolation if it gives you intimacy with the Creator of the Universe?

Intimacy with God is where divine revelation lives and breathes.

INTIMACY = REVELATION

There is a certain degree of revelation that comes along with walking intimately with God. Secrets, mysteries, hidden plans, concepts and ideas are revealed to the one who can be trusted with the weight of such revelation. The assignment that God has earmarked exclusively for you will require that you become laser-focused on Him.

How do you cultivate this type of intimacy? You know the usual suspects: reading the Word, praying & fasting. But what about:

- ○ sitting in silence so you can hear from Him

- creating a sacred space where you can meet with Him
- getting up early to meditate on His promises
- journaling your innermost thoughts
- writing Him a love song or singing one to Him

Can you think of any other ways to cultivate intimacy with God? _____

_____

David, who wrote some of his deepest devotions from the wilderness, highlights intimacy with God this way in Psalm 63:

O God, You *are* my God;
Early will I seek You; My soul thirsts for You; My
flesh longs for You in a dry and thirsty land
Where there is no water.
2 So I have looked for You in the sanctuary, To see Your power and Your glory.
3 Because Your lovingkindness *is* better than life, My lips shall praise You.
4 Thus I will bless You while I live; I will lift up my hands in Your name.
5 My soul shall be satisfied as with marrow and fatness,
And my mouth shall praise *You* with joyful lips.

What personal revelations do you glean from David's words?

_____

_____

DIG DEEPER

1 Corinthians 15:58
Therefore, my beloved brethren, be steadfast, immovable, always abounding in the work of the Lord, knowing that your labor is not in vain in the Lord.

S – SCRIPTURE

_____

_____

_____

E – EXAMINE

_____

_____

_____

E – ENVISION

_____

_____

_____

D – DECLARE

_____

_____

_____

DAY 3

"THE EPITOME OF GRACE"

Genesis 6:8-14

But Noah found grace in the eyes of the Lord.

9 This is the genealogy of Noah. Noah was a just man, perfect in his generations. Noah walked with God.

10 And Noah begot three sons: Shem, Ham, and Japheth.

11 The earth also was corrupt before God, and the earth was filled with violence.

12 So God looked upon the earth, and indeed it was corrupt; for all flesh had corrupted their way on the earth.

13 And God said to Noah, "The end of all flesh has come before Me, for the earth is filled with violence through them; and behold, I will destroy them with the earth.

14 Make yourself an ark of gopherwood; make rooms in the ark, and cover it inside and outside with pitch.

In verse 8 of Genesis 6, we see that Noah found grace in the eyes of the Lord. In between verses 13 and 14, we see another expression of God's grace. Although the words are not there, the evidence of grace is scattered in and throughout the text.

Read Genesis 6:13 and pause.

Then, read the first section of verse 14.

Did you see grace? God told Noah that the end of the earth was coming. Then, He said, *"make yourself an ark."* This is the epitome of grace poured out in Noah's life - - and in yours, if you'll open your eyes to see. Grace is living and breathing and occupying spaces that we cannot even fathom. It shows up in rooms that we've never entered. It lingers long after the dust has settled on our greatest disasters. It is one of the highest expressions of God's divine love.

Let's spend some time reflecting on this beautiful thing called grace…

Many believers are very familiar with the concept of grace. We talk about it, sing about it, and use it repeatedly in our prayers. This is perhaps the most used theological term in the New Testament. It is an awe-inspiring word that appears over 150 times in the New Testament alone. This word, *grace*, basically means a <u>divine favor given to people</u>[8]. And in the sense of New Testament theology, it is a divine favor given *to someone who could never earn it.*

Can you think of anything else that you've been given but did not earn? _____

In what ways have you experienced the grace of God in your own life? _____

_____

Grace defines our relationship with God. We are awakened from our spiritual sleep by a phenomenon that could only be called a work of grace. Undeserved favor.

We are
redeemed, regenerated, saved, sanctified, adopted,
justified, converted, born again…

(*pick whatever term you want to explain the spiritual transformation that has happened for every believer*) - - and then attach **'by grace'** to it. We are no more able to earn our way to spiritual maturity than we are to earn our way to salvation, that too is a work of grace. It is God's expression of favor, privilege, and blessing to His undeserving children.

And in the spirit of even more good news, God does not skimp on His grace. In fact, we are reminded in Ephesians chapter 2:4-7 that God blesses us according to the surpassing riches of His grace. **God's grace**, you might say, **is superabundant**.

Write Ephesians 2:8 here: _____

Luke said that the early Christians were experiencing (_____
_____) grace in Acts 4:33.

Paul informs us in Romans 5:2 that we all (_____)
in grace. We live in the environment of grace. It's the atmosphere in which we breathe spiritually.

And in Romans 5:17, he adds that God bestows upon us an (_____) of grace.

Draw a parallel between Paul's prayer in 2 Corinthians 12:7-9 and that of Jesus in Mark 14:32-41.

How many times did both Paul and Jesus pray?

_____

What was the outcome of each of their prayers?

_____

There is one problem that many of us have with grace…

When we are experiencing the worst of sufferings, trials, pain, discomfort and distress…

> No matter what you might think of grace; no matter how great, grand, lavish, or superabundant you think it is, James 4:6 adds, "But He gives more grace." It is greater than you think. It is greater than your mind can comprehend.

Instead of God removing the agony, He gives us more GRACE!

DIG DEEPER

Romans 6:14

For sin shall not have dominion over you, for you are not under law but under grace.

S – SCRIPTURE

_____

_____

_____

E – EXAMINE

_____

_____

_____

E – ENVISION

_____

_____

_____

D – DECLARE

_____

_____

_____

DAY 4

"THE REVELATION TO BUILD"

"Say it out loud: I NEED REVELATION"

God made an astonishing revelation to Noah - - there was so much sin, violence & wickedness on the earth, He would destroy the entire earth to rid it of evil. God gave Noah revelation of the assignment of a lifetime.

Genesis 6:13-22 ~ God gave Noah specific instructions … and "Noah did according to all that God commanded him (verse 22)."

Did you catch that? *Noah did according to all that God commanded him.*

Amos 3:7 - "Surely the Lord God does nothing, Unless He reveals His secret to His servants the prophets."

Jeremiah 33:3 - Call to me and I will answer you, and will tell you great and hidden things that you have not known.

Whatever God tells you to do … do it!

One of the greatest miracles in the Bible is Jesus turning water into wine at a wedding. When Mary, the mother of Jesus, was informed that the wedding party had run out of our wine, she turned to the servants and made a powerful statement: **"Whatever He says to you, do it**." (John 2:5)

> **Revelation 3:20** - Behold, I stand at the door and knock. If anyone hears my voice and opens the door, I will come in to him and eat with him, and he with me.

What is God telling you to do in this season of your life?

_____

Do it when you have all the answers - - and even when you don't.
Do it when you know all the details - - and even when everything is uncertain.
Do it when you're motivated - - and even when you're lazy.
Do it when it's perfect - - and while it's being perfected.
Do it when you're scared, lonely, unorganized, unsure, or anxious.
Just do it!

If you are going to build anything that stands the test of time, you need instructions - - but most importantly, you need divine revelation. The word "revelation" means a disclosure of what was previously unknown; the divine or supernatural disclosure to humans of something relating to human existence or the world[9].

Revelation is God making Himself known to mankind. It is a way of communication, by which God is the Communicator. In a theological context, there are two types of revelation: general (_or natural_) revelation and special (_or supernatural_) revelation. General (_or natural_) revelation says that God reveals Himself through nature by using our natural human make-up. We can observe the world around us and draw a logical conclusion that God exists. Nature itself speaks eloquently of its Creator. But, while mankind can know that God exists and even know the difference between good and evil - - nature alone does not make all of mankind a genuine believer.

In Paul's letter to the Romans, he said, *"For since the creation of the world His invisible attributes are clearly seen, being understood by the things that are made, even His eternal power and Godhead, so that they are without excuse, because, although they knew God, they did not glorify Him as God, nor were thankful, but became futile in their thoughts, and their foolish hearts were darkened."* (Romans 1:20-21)

In your own words, describe how these natural phenomena speak about God?

BY THIS:	YOU SEE THAT GOD IS:	BECAUSE THE BIBLE SAYS:
Weather (*storms, sunshine, rain, wind, etc.*)		Read Job 37:14-16
Physical landscape of the earth(*land, sea, sky, mountains, valleys, etc.*)		Read John 1:3
Living Beings (humans, animals, plants)		Read Job 12:7-10
Heaven and Earth		Read Psalm 96:11-12
Time and Seasons		Read Ecclesiastes 3:1-8

God uses nature, human reasoning and history to reveal Himself to humanity. But, there are many questions about God that man simply cannot figure out on his own – questions such as who God is, what sort of God He is, and His overall purpose in creating human beings. For these reasons, God has chosen to reveal Himself in a second, more *special* way. The second type of revelation is a special (or supernatural) revelation.

Special revelation is always supernatural in the way that God reveals Himself. God has revealed himself supernaturally in both events and word.[10] The events are reflective of God's interventions in human history.

God gave Noah an instruction: build!

Then, He gave him divine, supernatural revelation, which included the exact details on how to do it.

You cannot effectively complete your God-given assignment without revelation.
You can't grow a business without revelation.
You can't repair a relationship without revelation.
You can't be a purposeful parent without revelation.
You can't accomplish that goal without revelation.
You can't lead or serve effectively without revelation.
You can't build anything of significant value without revelation.

"Say it out loud: LORD, GIVE ME REVELATION!"

DIG DEEPER

Luke 8:17

"For nothing is secret that will not be revealed, nor anything hidden that will not be known and come to light."

S – SCRIPTURE

_____

_____

_____

E – EXAMINE

_____

_____

_____

E – ENVISION

_____

_____

_____

D – DECLARE

_____

_____

_____

DAY 5

"A COVENANT"

Genesis 6:18

But I will establish My covenant with you; and you shall go into the ark – you, your sons, your wife, and your sons' wives with you.

In contrast to everything that God revealed, Noah heard a new word: **covenant**. This is the first mention of "covenant" in the Scriptures. It was a promise from God that not only would Noah and his family be preserved, but they would enjoy the bountiful benefits of a covenant relationship with God.

Let's examine how the author of Hebrews 8 paints a distinction between the first covenant and the new covenant:

fill in the blank using the (NKJV) translation

For if that _____ had been faultless, then no place would have been sought for a _____. ⁸Because finding fault with them, He says: "Behold, the days are coming, says the Lord, when I will make a _____ with the house of Israel and with the house of Judah— ⁹not according to _____ that I made with their fathers in the day when I took them by the hand to lead them out of the land of Egypt; because they did not continue in _____, and I disregarded them, says the Lord. ¹⁰ For this *is* _____ that I will make with the house of Israel after those days, says the Lord: I will put My laws in their mind and write them on their hearts; and I will be their God, and they shall be My people. ¹¹ None of them shall teach his neighbor, and none his brother, saying, 'Know the Lord,' for all shall know Me, from the least of them to the greatest of them. ¹² For I will be merciful to their unrighteousness, and their sins and their lawless deeds I will remember no more."

¹³ In that He says, "_____," He has made the first obsolete. Now what is becoming obsolete and growing old is ready to vanish away.

Historically, the first covenant was made with Noah (Genesis 6:18). The *old* covenant always refers to the Mosaic Covenant or the Covenant of the Law (Exodus 19:1 – 20:21). By nature, the Covenant of the Law was primarily external, which is why the Hebrews author (*quoting from Jeremiah 31:31-34*) said that the Lord would '*put My laws in their mind and write them on their hearts*'.

| The 5 Covenants of Scripture ||
NAME OF COVENANT	SCRIPTURE(S)
Noahic	Genesis 9:8-17
Abrahamic	Genesis 15:12-21
Mosaic	Exodus 19:5-6
Davidic	2 Samuel 7:4-17
New	Jeremiah 31:31-34

The New Covenant, which is sealed by the shed blood of Jesus Christ, is an internal occurrence.

Ezekiel 36:26 points to the promise of conversion and spiritual renewal that would be made available in the New Covenant. Write the words to this verse below:

_____

The gift of the "new heart" signifies the new birth, which is regeneration by the Holy Spirit. The "heart" stands for the whole nature of a person. The "spirit" signifies the governing power of the mind, which directs thought and behavior. This New Covenant conversion is only made possible by the atonement of Jesus Christ.

> Genesis 6:14 – Make yourself an ark of gopherwood; make rooms in the ark, and cover it inside and outside with pitch.

You should know that God had a covenant in mind when He instructed Noah in Genesis 6:14 to 'cover it (*the ark*) inside and outside with pitch'. There's an interesting juxtaposition happening in this one statement - - pointing to the fact that God had already made plans for Noah's redemption. Noah was to seal the boat with **pitch**. The root word for pitch is kâphar, (*pronounced kaw-fa*) which is the Hebrew word for ransom (and **atonement**)[11]. Holman Illustrated Bible Dictionary defines atonement as the biblical doctrine that God has reconciled sinners to Himself through the sacrificial work of Jesus Christ[12]. The concept of atonement spans both Testaments, everywhere pointing to the death, burial, and resurrection of Jesus for the sins of the world.

Look up the definition of atonement in any dictionary. Below, include more synonyms (or related words) for atonement.

	redemption
	payment
Atonement	

On the cross, Jesus absorbed the wrath of God. It was a holy transaction between Father and Son. The Father poured out His anger towards sin onto Jesus, and His wrath was ultimately and eternally satisfied. Because of that, the guilty sinner who trusts in Christ is set free from the penalty of sin and is reconciled to God. Hallelujah!

Knowing that He was sending Noah into the storm of a lifetime, God's covenant specified an element that would work as a binding agent to waterproof the boat: **pitch**!

Eight people survived the Flood of a lifetime because God told Noah to use pitch. It was the very thing that would anchor the ark from the inside out.

NEXT WEEK:
After Noah received the "revelation to build" - - which were the details of building out the Ark, it was 120 years before he stepped foot on what he had built. Next week, we will talk about "the waiting season." What do you do while you wait?!

There was another life-saving miracle involving the use of pitch. Read Exodus 2:3 and write down the materials that Moses's mother used to waterproof the boat.

DIG DEEPER

Psalm 65:3

Iniquities prevail against me; as for our transgressions, You will provide atonement for them.

S – SCRIPTURE

_____

_____

_____

E – EXAMINE

_____

_____

_____

E – ENVISION

_____

_____

_____

D – DECLARE

_____

_____

_____

WEEK 4

WAIT

DAY 1

"WAIT AT THE DOOR"

What do you do when you've followed God's instructions exactly and nothing happened?

What do you do when you've sacrificed your all and no one even noticed?

What do you do when you've prayed & fasted and the answer still hasn't come?

What do you do when you've been in a long and drawn-out season of waiting?

What do you do when everything around you seems dormant?

What do you do when God makes you wait?

In Genesis 6, we learned that Noah walked with God. This level of intimacy set Noah apart from everybody else on the earth. Because of this, God gave Noah the divine revelation that He was going to destroy the earth and everything on it, but Noah and his family would be saved. God gave Noah specific instructions for building the ark. How tall, how long, how wide, how many windows…but there would only be **one door** (Genesis 6:16).

Why do you think there was only one door?

_____

Let's take some clues from John 10:

> John 10:7-9 – Then Jesus said to them again, "Most assuredly, I say to you, I am the door of the sheep. All who ever came before Me are thieves and robbers, but the sheep did not hear them. I am the door. If anyone enters by Me, he will be saved, and will go in and out and find pasture."

Jesus's words echoed the same sentiments in John 14:6. Write down what He said:

_____

These statements are referred to as the I AM statements of Jesus. There are 7 of them found in the book of John. Let's fill in the others:

I AM STATEMENT	VERSE
	John 6:48
	John 8:12
I am the door	John 10:7,9
	John 10:11
	John 11:25
I am the way, the truth, and the life	John 14:6
	John 15:1,5

Noah went about his work, building the ark. Then he waited. The span of time between Noah building the ark and the first drops of rainfall was 120 years (Genesis 6:3).

1 Peter 3:20 ~ 'who formerly were disobedient, when once the Divine long-suffering waited in the days of Noah, while the ark was being prepared, in which a few, that is, eight souls, were saved through water.'

In this passage, Peter explained that Hell is inhabited by bound demons who have been there since the time of Noah and who were sent there because they severely overstepped the boundaries of God's tolerance with their wickedness. The demons of Noah's day were running riot through the earth, filling the world with their wicked, vile, anti-God activity, so that even 120 years of Noah's preaching - - while the ark was being built - - could not convince any of humanity to believe in God.

Noah preached anyway…and he waited. For 120 years.

Noah was waiting on a "Flood" that he'd never experienced before. He had zero details about floods; what it looked like, felt like, or sounded like. Yet, he stood at the door of history with a hope that was surely uncommon and anticipation that was unshakeable. And he waited.

What door are you waiting on God to open? _____

Do you see any significance in your waiting? If so, what? _____

What are you learning about God and/or yourself while you wait? _____

DIG DEEPER

S-E-E-D VERSE:

Psalm 27:14

Wait on the Lord; be of good courage, and He shall strengthen your heart; wait, I say, on the Lord!

S – SCRIPTURE

_____

_____

_____

E – EXAMINE

_____

_____

_____

E – ENVISION

_____

_____

_____

D – DECLARE

_____

_____

_____

DAY 2

"TEACH ME TO WAIT WELL"

We spend a lot of our time waiting. Waiting in line. Waiting for news. Waiting for someone to apologize. Waiting for the pain to subside. Waiting for the perfect time. Waiting for the next season of life. Waiting until we have all the answers, resources, or whatever we feel is needed to justify the wait.

We don't know how Noah felt waiting to enter that Ark, but one thing is for sure, we all know what waiting feels like.

Waiting is hard. Often uncomfortable. Seemingly unnecessary.

But **waiting with purpose** is worth it. We must remember that God is still at work, even in our waiting.

Noah is not the only biblical hero who waited on rain. Let's visit the story of Elijah in 1 Kings 18. Coming off the heels of one of the greatest displays of God's power in his ministry (*where God put the idols and prophets of Baal to an open shame*), Elijah prayed for rain.

1 Kings 18:41-46 – Elijah prays for rain

Then Elijah said to Ahab, "Go up, eat and drink; for *there is* the sound of abundance of rain." 42 So Ahab went up to eat and drink. And Elijah went up to the top of Carmel; then he bowed down on the ground, and put his face between his knees, 43 and said to his servant, "Go up now, look toward the sea."

So he went up and looked, and said, "*There is* nothing." And seven times he said, "Go again."

44 Then it came to pass the seventh *time,* that he said, "There is a cloud, as small as a man's hand, rising out of the sea!" So he said, "Go up, say to Ahab, 'Prepare *your chariot,* and go down before the rain stops you.'"

45 Now it happened in the meantime that the sky became black with clouds and wind, and there was a heavy rain. So Ahab rode away and went to Jezreel. 46 Then the hand of the Lord came upon Elijah; and he girded up his loins and ran ahead of Ahab to the entrance of Jezreel.

Facing a severe famine and drought, but armed with a promise from God, Elijah prayed for rain.

In verse 42 above, draw a circle ar-ound the position that Elijah took when he prayed.

Elijah provides one of the most signifi-cant illustrations of the power of prayer

JAMES 5:17-18 ~ Elijah was a man with a nature like ours, and he prayed earnestly that it would not rain; and it did not rain on the land for three years and six months. 18 And he prayed again, and the heaven gave rain, and the earth produced its fruit.

in the OT. His prayers both initiated and ended a long-awaited drought of 3 ½ years.

He *'bowed down on the ground, and put his face between his knees'*. Elijah assumed the position of a woman in labor. This is indicative of a travailing type of prayer. Jesus made mention of this figurative language in John 16:21. Write down His words from the King James version of Scripture:

_____

Labor pains are an indication that birth will soon follow. Whether Elijah felt the physical pains of birth or not, he positioned himself to bring forth the very thing God had already promised him: rain!

Elijah asked his servant to check for rain again, and again, and again - - for a total of seven times (*which is the number of completion*). Many of us would have given up by the 3rd or 4th time because there were no signs of rain coming.

Why do you think Elijah was so persistent?

_____

On the 7th time, Elijah's servant returned with news - - there was a cloud! Please do not overlook the fact that the *size* of the cloud is mentioned here. Why do you think that was an important piece of information for Elijah?

_____

Isaiah 66:7-9 - Before she was in labor, she gave birth; before her pain came, she delivered a male child.

Who has heard such a thing? Who has seen such things? Shall the earth be made to give birth in one day? Or shall a nation be born at once? For as soon as Zion was in labor, she gave birth to her children.

Shall I bring to the time of birth, and not cause delivery?" says the LORD. "Shall I who cause delivery shut up *the womb*?" says your God.

How often do we overlook what God is doing in our lives because it is not packaged in the way we expect it? That's a rhetorical question, of course. Although it was only the size of a man's hand, the cloud was evidence of the rain that Elijah had prayed for.

Did you catch that word: **evidence**? Notice that Elijah didn't wait for the actual rain to appear. Once he heard the news that a cloud had formed, it was all the evidence he needed. Rain was coming. And not just any kind of rain. A torrential downpour.

What did Elijah send his servant to tell Ahab? _____

What evidence are you currently waiting on? _____

The truth is that the evidence of God's faithfulness is locked and loaded throughout His Word. In fact, Jesus pronounced a special blessing on you (yes, you!) because you have believed without seeing, without evidence. (John 20:29)

> Jesus said to him, "Thomas, because you have seen Me, you have believed. Blessed *are* those who have not seen and *yet* have believed."

If He promised it, He will always follow through - - but sometimes you must wait. Perhaps you don't need more evidence - - you simply need to have faith that God hears you and He will answer.

Waiting is not an inactive disposition, where you do nothing.

While you wait, pray. Fervently. Persistently. With confidence and authority. With assurance and boldness.

1 John 5:14-15
Now this is the confidence that we have in Him, that if we ask anything according to His will, He hears us. 15 And if we know that He hears us, whatever we ask, we know that we have the petitions that we have asked of Him.

Pray this:

Lord, teach me how to wait well.

Now, spend some time today meditating on these truths:

HOW TO WAIT WELL:

- With the soul - Psalm 62:1, 5 - **"Truly my soul silently waits for God; From Him comes my salvation. He only is my rock and my salvation; He is my defense; I shall not be greatly moved." "My soul, wait silently for God alone, For my expectation is from Him."**
- With earnest desire - Psalm 130:6
- With patience - Psalm 37:7, **Psalm 40:1 - "I waited patiently for the Lord, and He inclined to me, and heard my cry."**
- With full confidence - Micah 7:7
- Continually - Hosea 12:6
- All day - Psalm 25:5
- Especially in adversity - Psalm 59:1-9, Isaiah 8:17
- With hope in His word - Psalm 130:5

DIG DEEPER

S-E-E-D VERSE:

Psalm 130:5

I wait for the LORD, my soul waits, And in His word I do hope.

S – SCRIPTURE

_____

_____

_____

E – EXAMINE

_____

_____

_____

E – ENVISION

_____

_____

_____

D – DECLARE

_____

_____

_____

DAY 3

"WORK + WAIT"

Hebrews 11:7 – By faith Noah, being divinely warned of things not yet seen, moved with godly fear, prepared an ark for the saving of his household, by which he condemned the world and became heir of the righteousness which is according to faith.

One of the key turning points in Noah's story is that he '*moved with godly fear*' to build something that had never been built - - for a worldwide flood that had never been experienced. Noah went to work. Although Scripture does not mention Noah's occupation (other than a '*preacher of righteousness*' - 2 Peter 2:5), it is safe to say that he wasn't a sailor. We also don't know whether he had experience in shipbuilding. Even if he did, the skill set that would have been required to build a vessel to the proportions that God outlined was unheard of. Whatever the case, we can be confident that God made sure Noah was fully equipped for the task at hand. In the same way, when God calls any of us to an assignment, we can trust that He will prepare, equip and anoint us accordingly. (Philippians 1:6, Hebrews 13:21)

God does not oftentimes call the qualified.
He qualifies those whom He has called.

Draw a line to match these modern-day occupations with the skills/responsibilities that were divinely given to Noah:

Veterinarian   Spread the News about a Flood to a Faithless Generation

Shipbuilder   Navigate the Ark through the Flood of a Lifetime

Meteorologist   Collect & Prepare the Proper Foods for 100s of Different Animals

Sailor   Collect, Feed and Care for Animals

Dietician   Build an Ark that would rival any Modern-Day Cargo Ship

Preacher   Determine the Weather and Post-Flood Conditions

The size of the Ark in modern-day measurements were 450 feet long, 75 feet wide and 45 feet high. The shape was equivalent to a gigantic box with three floors, one window and one door (Genesis 6:16). Bible scholars have calculated that approximately 45,000 animals may have fit on the Ark. A vessel of this magnitude likely required skilled workers during the construction process. Although Scripture does not identify who (*or how many people*) aided Noah in building the Ark, it is telling that not even one of them felt convicted to join him in the Ark.

Have you ever embarked upon an assignment with both faith and fear? Look up the definition of **courage** and write it below.

_____

Courage is the level of *godly fear* that you will often have to walk in - - where you're scared out of your wits, confronted with mountains of criticism, overwhelmed with uncertainty, but you press on anyway.

Read Joshua 1:1-9.

Record how many times you see the words 'strong and courageous'.
Why do you think Joshua needed strength and courage? _____

Now, read Deuteronomy 31:1-8 and make a note of the words Moses uses to encourage Joshua. In verse 3, who does Moses say would cross over Jordan first? _____

There is a principle for faith and confidence being echoed throughout these two passages of Scripture. In the latter part of Joshua 1:9 and Deuteronomy 31:6,8 why should Joshua have confidence in the assignment he is undertaking? _____

After 120 years of working (*with godly fear*), preaching (*with godly fear*), and waiting (*with godly fear*), the time had finally come.

What could you accomplish if you had Noah's version of *godly fear*? _____

Genesis 7:1 - **"Then the Lord said to Noah, 'Come into the ark, you and your household, because I have seen that you are righteous before Me in this generation.'**

DIG DEEPER

James 5:8
You also be patient. Establish your hearts, for the coming of the Lord is at hand.

S – SCRIPTURE

_____

_____

_____

E – EXAMINE

_____

_____

_____

E – ENVISION

_____

_____

_____

D – DECLARE

_____

_____

_____

DAY 4

"WHEN TESTS COME"

After all the years of waiting, Noah and his family finally enter the Ark. (Genesis 7:1). Surely, this was the moment that he had been anticipating. And yet again, he must wait. Seven more days of angst, uncertainty, and waiting. Perhaps it was to allow Noah and his family to get more acquainted with the Ark. Perhaps it was to allow more time for sinners to repent. Whatever the reason, God put him on hold once again.

> **Genesis 7:4** – *For after seven more days I will cause it to rain on the earth forty days and forty nights, and I will destroy from the face of the earth all living things that I have made.*

If you are in a waiting season, you're in good company. Let's take a peek at how God used a *wait* for His glory…

Who?	Waiting on what?	Scripture Reference	Find the key words from the Scripture	Write your observations below
Abraham	For a promise to be fulfilled	Hebrews 6:13-15	What did he do in verse 15?	Patiently endured, obtained the promise
Joseph	In Prison for his purpose to be revealed	Genesis 50:19-20	What was the result of all he had experienced (*see the last words in verse 20*)?	
David	To be king	1 Samuel 16:13	When did he become king over all Israel (*see 2 Samuel 5:3-4*)?	
Daniel	For prayers to be answered	Daniel 10:12-13	When were his prayers heard (*see verse 12*)?	
Jesus	To begin His ministry	Luke 3:21-23	What age did He begin His ministry (*see verse 23*)?	

Look back at Genesis 7:1. What is the first word God spoke to Noah in this verse?

_____

'Come into the Ark' is a powerful revelation we shouldn't miss. It is a beautiful reminder that Noah was not entering a secluded and lonely Ark. In fact, God was already there - - extending an invitation to join Him in a place that had been hollowed out specifically for Noah. The Ark was a refuge (*which is defined as protection or shelter, as from danger or hardship*)[13].

Maybe this is exactly what David had in mind when he penned the words to Psalm 91. In verses 1-2, what connections do you make between Noah and David?

He who dwells in the _____ of the Most High God shall _____ under the _____ of the Almighty. I will say of the Lord, "He is my _____ and my _____; My God in Him I will _____."

Although David's metaphoric language is likened to an army preparing for battle, Noah was entering his own type of battle. One where trust in God would reign supreme. One where fear of the unknown would subside. One where obedience would dominate. And one where the victory has already been secured.

WHEN GOD MAKES YOU WAIT, HERE ARE SOME PROMISES:

- You are heard - Psalm 40:1
- You are blessed - Isaiah 30:18
- You experience His goodness - Lamentations 3:25
- You will not be ashamed - Psalm 25:3, Isaiah 49:23
- Your strength will be renewed - Isaiah 40:31
- You will inherit the earth - Psalm 37:9
- You will be saved - Proverbs 20:22, Isaiah 25:9
- You will receive the glorious things God has prepared for you – Isaiah 64:4

Continue reading Psalm 91, making a note of the protection that has been promised to the believer. Observe how, regardless of the dangers or terrors, the righteous can rest in the Lord. Allow the truths of Scripture to quiet your fears, comfort your heart and give you peace.

What conclusions do you draw from Psalm 91 that minister to you personally?

_____

DIG DEEPER

S-E-E-D VERSE:

Psalm 37:9

For evildoers shall be cut off; but those who wait on the Lord, they shall inherit the earth.

S – SCRIPTURE

_____

_____

_____

E – EXAMINE

_____

_____

_____

E – ENVISION

_____

_____

_____

D – DECLARE

_____

_____

_____

DAY 5

"THE LORD SHUT HIM IN"

Genesis 7:16. "So those that entered, male and female of all flesh, went in as God had commanded him; and the Lord shut him in."

Today, we arrive at a crucial point in the story. After decades of preparing, working and waiting, Noah (along with his family and the animals) enter the Ark.

Circle the last 6 words of the above verse.

Why do you think it's important to understand that Noah didn't close the door himself?

_____

and the Lord shut him in - -

This statement reveals several things:

1. That Noah and all those aboard were recipients of divine care and protection
2. That Noah's obedience was crucial to everyone embarking the Ark
3. That God Himself is credited with sealing the boat
4. That the salvation from judgment and the preservation of life was God's doing, not Noah's

Look up the definition of **judgment** and write it below.

_____

According to Ephesians 2:1, what do believers receive as a result of salvation, as opposed to judgment? _____

According to Ephesians 2:4, there are 2 reasons why we are 'made alive'. What are they?

_____

Genesis 7:16 is also a foreshadow of the ultimate salvation made available to those who accept Jesus Christ as their Lord and Savior. The Ark portrays our salvation in Christ - - He is the Ark of salvation. In John 10:9 Jesus says, "*I am the door. If anyone enters by Me, he will be saved, and will go in and out and find pasture.*" Jesus is the only *door* by which we enter into salvation.

Genesis 6:20 makes note that Noah didn't have to spend his time gathering and corralling all the animals. He didn't have to track them down. Noah didn't have to concern himself with the details of God's plan.

That's God's business!

The latter part of Genesis 6:20 (two of every *kind* will come to you to keep *them* alive, emphasis added) is evidence that God will oversee every single detail of His plan. Obedience to Him - - now that's *your* responsibility.

Man's responsibility → versus → God's sovereignty

According to Romans 10:9, what is man's responsibility? _____

As a result of man's responsibility, what is God's sovereignty? _____

According to Ephesians 2:4-8, what is man's responsibility? _____

As a result of man's responsibility, what is God's sovereignty? _____

Furthermore, Scripture teaches that we '*have been sealed with the Holy Spirit of promise*'. (Ephesians 1:13) This seal authenticates our salvation with security, ownership and authority. The Holy Spirit indwells the believer with an airtight, tamper-proof seal for all eternity.

From Ephesians 1, explore the spiritual blessings that are abundant in Christ.

Chosen in Him before _____ that we should be ___ and _____ before Him (verse 4)

In Him, we have _____ (verse 7)
In Him, we have _____ (verse 8)
In Him, you were _____ (verse 13)

As we close out this week of study, take some time to reflect on the S-E-E-D verses that have been covered. As you think about the waiting seasons of your own life, which of these verses give you the most encouragement right now?

_____

DIG DEEPER

John 1:17

For the law was given through Moses, but grace and truth came through Jesus Christ.

S – SCRIPTURE

_____

_____

_____

E – EXAMINE

_____

_____

_____

E – ENVISION

_____

_____

_____

D – DECLARE

_____

_____

_____

THE FLOOD CHRONOLOGY[14]

Timeline (days)	Duration	Month/Day	Description	Bible Reference
0	Initial reference point	600th year of Noah's life: 2nd month, 17th day of the month	The fountains of the great deep broke apart and the windows of heaven were opened; it began to rain. This happened on the seventeenth day of the second month. Noah actually entered the Ark seven days prior to this.	Genesis 7:11
40	40 days and nights	3rd month, 27th day of the month	Rain fell for 40 days, and then water covered the earth's highest places (at that time) by over ~20 feet (15 cubits) and began the stage of flooding until the next milestone.	Genesis 7:11–12, Genesis 7:17–20
150	150 days (including the initial 40 days)	7th month, 17th day of the month	The water rose to its highest level (covering the whole earth) sometime between the 40th and 150th day, and the end of these 150 days was the seventeenth day of the seventh month. The Ark rested on the mountains of Ararat. On the 150th day, the springs of the great deep were shut off, and the rain from above ceased, and the water began continually receding.	Genesis 7:24–8:5
150 + 74 = 224	74 days	10th month, 1st day of the month	The tops of the mountains became visible on the tenth month, first day.	Genesis 8:5

224 + 40 = 264	40 days	11th month, 11th day of the month	After 40 more days, Noah sent out a raven.	Genesis 8:6
264 + 7 = 271	7 days	11th month, 18th day of the month	The dove was sent out seven days after the raven. It had no resting place and returned to Noah.	Genesis 8:6–12
271 + 7 = 278	7 days	11th month, 25th day of the month	After seven more days, Noah sent out the dove again. It returned again but this time with an olive leaf in its beak.	Genesis 8:10–11
278 + 7 = 285	7 days	12th month, 2nd day of the month	After seven more days, Noah sent out the dove again, and it did not return.	Genesis 8:12
314	29 days	601st year of Noah life: 1st month, 1st day of the month	Noah removed the cover of the Ark on the first day of the first month. The *surface* of the earth was dried up, and Noah could verify this to the extent of what he could see.	Genesis 8:13
370 (371 if counting the first day and last day as full days)	56 days	2nd month, 27th day of the month	The *earth* was dry, and God commanded Noah's family and the animals to come out of the Ark. From the first day of the year during the daylight portion there were 29.5 more days left in the month plus 26.5 more days left in the second month until the exit.	Genesis 8:14–17, Genesis 7:11

WEEK 5

THE ANCHOR

DAY 1

"A MOMENT OF SILENCE"

Genesis 7:17-24 ~ Now the flood was on the earth forty days. The waters increased and lifted up the ark, and it rose high above the earth. **18** The waters prevailed and greatly increased on the earth, and the ark moved about on the surface of the waters. **19** And the waters prevailed exceedingly on the earth, and all the high hills under the whole heaven were covered. **20** The waters prevailed fifteen cubits upward, and the mountains were covered. **21** And all flesh died that moved on the earth: birds and cattle and beasts and every creeping thing that creeps on the earth, and every man. **22** All in whose nostrils *was* the breath of the spirit of life, all that *was* on the dry *land,* died. **23** So He destroyed all living things which were on the face of the ground: both man and cattle, creeping thing and bird of the air. They were destroyed from the earth. Only Noah and those who *were* with him in the ark remained *alive*. **24** And the waters prevailed on the earth one hundred and fifty days.

Can we take a moment of silence for what we just read?
Can we take a moment of silence for every land-dwelling, air-breathing *creature and human* that perished?
Can we take a moment of silence for the 8 surviving souls aboard the Ark?
Can we take a moment of silence for God's judgment?

> Genesis 7:11-24 describes the greatest disaster the world has ever known. For forty days and nights, rain fell from the windows of heaven above, and the underground fountains of water gushed from below. As a result, floodwaters fully covered the surface of the earth for another 110 days. The ark, built as God instructed Noah, survived the deluge. All creatures and humans perished, except for those on-board.

What thoughts and feelings come to mind when you reflect on how God used the Flood to bring judgment to the earth?

_____

Psalm 46:10 - Be still, and know that I am God

Today, let's practice stillness. First, write in the definition of stillness. _____

_____

Psalm 46 launches a trilogy of psalms (46, 47 and 48) as songs of triumph which have been regarded as the "songs of Zion." In Psalm 46:1-3, the poetic language that the psalmist uses lends

"Sitting on that boat while the water surged on the earth 150 days (Genesis 7:24), Noah's family acted as a living reminder that God who fiercely judges sin is the same one who, through our faith, mercifully delivers us from it."[15]

itself to a revelation that is worth exploring. *'Even though the earth be removed, and the mountains be carried into the midst of the sea'* alludes to a natural disaster, similar to an earthquake. But, these fixtures in nature represent symbols of stability. When you think about 'the earth' and the 'mountains,' you probably think of their grandeur, strength and fortitude - - they are permanent, *still,* elements in our world that are not easily moved.

In the stillness of this moment, think about what has moved you. As you reflect over the last 2 years, what has caused you the most unrest?

Most people have an innate desire for stability. It is what we deem as a necessary, non-negotiable in life. We want stability in our careers, relationships, health, finances, home and family life, etc. But what happens when the things we have regarded as *stable* become unstable, unreliable, and uncertain? Psalm 46:2 reminds us that when the earth is shaken and when mountains move, or tremble, or stagger, or slip, the believer has "no fear" because of the unchangeableness of our God.

As you sit in stillness today, meditate on the truth of Hebrews 13:8 (*Jesus Christ is the same yesterday, to-day and forever.*) and what it means to your personal, deep-seated desire for stability.

> Although God used the rain to judge the sins of the world, rain is most often seen as a blessing in the Scriptures.

- I will give you rain in due season. (Leviticus 26:4)
- My doctrine shall drop as the rain. (Deuteronomy 32:2)
- No rain because they have sinned. (1 Kings 8:35-36)
- Who *gives* rain on the earth. (Job 5:10)
- Who prepares rain for the earth. (Psalm 147:8)
- Favor is a cloud of the latter rain. (Proverbs 16:15)
- Lord our God that giveth rain. (Jeremiah 5:24)
- *Ask* ye of the Lord for rain in the time of the latter rain. (Zechariah 10:1)

DIG DEEPER

Isaiah 26:3

You will keep him in perfect peace, whose mind is stayed on You, because he trusts in You.

S – SCRIPTURE

_____

_____

_____

E – EXAMINE

_____

_____

_____

E – ENVISION

_____

_____

_____

D – DECLARE

_____

_____

_____

DAY 2

"THE SILENT TEACHER"

After Noah entered the Ark, God did not speak until the Flood was over and the *earth was dried*' (Genesis 8:14). No more instructions. No more revelations. No still, small voice of reassurance. Just silence.

Noah was being tested in ways that he could have never imagined. Although his name would end up being mentioned amongst the great fathers of our faith (Hebrews 11), this period of isolation was yet another test of Noah's own faith.

What do you do when God is silent during the seemingly greatest test of your life?

From beginning to end, the rain and subsequent Flood lasted one year and fifty days, from Genesis 7:11 to Genesis 8:14. We see many details about the Flood. But we don't see God. Nor do we hear Him.

Why do you think God was silent? _____

There's a definition of isolation that paints a broader picture. It is defined as- the condition of being concealed or hidden[16]. Noah entered the Ark *with* God. Then, he was isolated - - secluded, separated, quarantined - - for over a year because God had yet another assignment waiting on him.

Don't misjudge a season of isolation. God will hide you on purpose. When you go through seasons of isolation, instead of getting in your feelings, try this: get in the presence of God. Oftentimes, He wants to speak to you and isolation is the only way to get your attention. Shut the door, turn off your phone, silence your mind - - ABBA Father wants to commune with you.

In what ways have you experienced God's presence during seasons of isolation?

_____

When the Teacher is silent, there are a few things you need to know.

1) Know that the test has a purpose.

God is building something inside of you that can't be seen with the naked eye.

> **James 1:2-4** ~ My brethren, count it all joy when you fall into various trials, knowing that the testing of your faith produces patience. But let patience have *its* perfect work, that you may be perfect and complete, lacking nothing.

2) Know that silence doesn't mean absence.

("Footprints in the Sand"[17])

One night I dreamed a dream. As I was walking along the beach with my Lord. Across the dark sky flashed scenes from my life. For each scene, I noticed two sets of footprints in the sand, One belonging to me and one to my Lord.

After the last scene of my life flashed before me, I looked back at the footprints in the sand. I noticed that at many times along the path of my life, especially at the very lowest and saddest times, there was only one set of footprints.

This really troubled me, so I asked the Lord about it. "Lord, you said once I decided to follow you, You'd walk with me all the way. But I noticed that during the saddest and most troublesome times of my life, there was only one set of footprints. I don't understand why, when I needed You the most, You would leave me."

He whispered, "My precious child, I love you and will never leave you, Never, ever, during your trials and testings. When you saw only one set of footprints, It was then that I carried you."

Hebrews 13:5 - For He Himself has said, "I will never leave you nor forsake you."

3) Know that God is working even when He seems silent.

What is God doing in your midst that you may have failed to see?

Are you looking for God from the vantage point that has been disappointed by the seasons of isolation? Or the frustration with seeing other people get or do the very thing you're praying for? Or from the lens of failed attempts at success? Or the discouragement that is knocking at your soul?

Habakkuk the prophet, prayed, *"O LORD, how long shall I cry, and You will not hear? Even cry out to You, "Violence!" and You will not save.* (Habakkuk 1:2)

Habakkuk prayed 2 questions: How long? and Why?

When God responded (because God always responds, whether we are tuned in or not), He told Habakkuk to: *"Look among the nations and watch – Be utterly astounded! For I will work a work in your days which you would not believe, though it were told you."* (Habakkuk 1:5)

God broke the silence with these 3 proclamations:

- **Look** - - with your spiritual eyes that have been sharpened by the knowledge of who you are in Christ
- **Watch** - - sit up and pay close attention; don't miss any details
- **Be utterly astounded** - - be literally dumbfounded; filled with amazement and surprise

God concluded with *"For I will work a work in your days which you would not believe, though it were told you."*

Essentially, He was saying - - "Chill out! I am working in ways that you cannot even fathom. I am moving behind the scenes, working in the silent seasons of your life, performing miracles that have never been thought of. If I showed you every detail of what I'm doing, it would blow your mind. I do my best work in silence."

If you have experienced seasons where God seemed silent, what did you learn about yourself in the process?

_____

DIG DEEPER

John 10:27
My sheep hear my voice. I know them, and they follow me.

S – SCRIPTURE

_____

_____

_____

E – EXAMINE

_____

_____

_____

E – ENVISION

_____

_____

_____

D – DECLARE

_____

_____

DAY 3

"GOD NEVER FORGETS"

Genesis 8:1-5 ~ Then God remembered Noah, and every living thing, and all the animals that *were* with him in the ark. And God made a wind to pass over the earth, and the waters subsided. **2** The fountains of the deep and the windows of heaven were also stopped, and the rain from heaven was restrained. **3** And the waters receded continually from the earth. At the end of the hundred and fifty days the waters decreased. **4** Then the ark rested in the seventh month, the seventeenth day of the month, on the mountains of Ararat. **5** And the waters decreased continually until the tenth month. In the tenth *month*, on the first *day* of the month, the tops of the mountains were seen.

Have you ever prayed for something so long, wanted it so desperately, yearned for it so deeply that you forgot just how long you'd been waiting for it? Have you ever gone weeks, months or even years believing for a breakthrough? Have you ever gotten lost in a long-awaited promise? Have you ever wondered whether God has forgotten?

The first 4 words of Genesis 8:1 can strike some of us as disturbing. *Then God remembered Noah.* It can be troubling to think that perhaps God had been so busy bringing judgment to the world, destroying every living thing in its path, that He'd forgotten about Noah. Rest assured, God never forgets. This word 'remembered' is not indicative of a flaw in God's character. It is an anthropomorphic term often used in the Bible to describe God in human language that we can understand. The root word for 'remembered' is *zākar.* It

> Isaiah 49:15-16 ~ "Can a woman forget her nursing child,
> And not have compassion on the son of her womb?
> Surely they may forget,
> Yet I will not forget you.
> **16** See, I have inscribed you on the palms *of My hands;*
> Your walls *are* continually before Me.

means to bring to mind; to collect thoughts in a piercing and penetrating manner[18]. God made a covenant with Noah - - one that could never be forgotten. And the thought of that covenant was brought to the forefront of His mind.

> Psalm 105:8 ~ He remembers His covenant forever,
> The word *which* He commanded, for a thousand generations

Describe a significant time in your life when it seemed as if God had forgotten about you? _____
Where did you find reassurance? _____

Let's take a stroll down memory lane to see the covenant-keeping power of God…

God didn't forget about Abraham & Sarah. He fulfilled His promise to them. (Genesis 21:1-2)

God didn't forget about Hagar. He pronounced a blessing on her and her son. (Genesis 21:17-18)

God didn't forget about Rachel. He opened up her womb. (Genesis 30:22)

God didn't forget about the children of Israel. He brought them out of bondage again and again. (Exodus 2:24)

God didn't forget about Daniel in the lion's den. He shut the lion's mouth. (Daniel 6:22)

God didn't forget about Jonah in the belly of the fish. He commanded the fish to spit Jonah out onto dry land. (Jonah 2:10)

God didn't forget about Job. He restored everything Job lost two times over. (Job 42:10)

God didn't forget about Lazarus. He resurrected him after being dead for four days. (John 11:43)

Just as God remembered the saints of old, He will remember you. As a matter of fact, He's thinking about you right now. Your dreams, your desires, your flaws, your well-being, your purpose, your heart, your truth. And, if you can hold onto the promise that He has not forgotten about you, it will bring you comfort and hope when you want to give up.

Not only has God not forgotten about you, but every tear that has soaked your pillow at night, He has collected.

Read the below verse and record what you see in these words:

> Psalm 56:8 ~ You number my wanderings;
> Put my tears into Your bottle;
> *Are they* not in Your book?

_____

Now, read the same verse in a different Bible translation, preferably a paraphrased version such as The Message Bible or The Passion Translation.

Which *book* do you think David was referring to in the above verse? _____

The last work in the Minor Prophets comes to a close in the book of Malachi. God seals the Old Testament canon both historically and prophetically. Malachi wrote the final prophecy of the OT, delivering God's message of judgment on Israel for their perpetual sin and God's promise of future redemption through the coming Messiah. There would be 400 years of divine silence before another prophet arrives with a message from God. Preaching in the wilderness, John the Baptist proclaimed, "Repent, for the Kingdom of heaven is at hand!" (Matthew 3:2). The Messiah has come.

Read Malachi 3:16 and record the everlasting promise to 'those who feared the LORD.'

_____

God never forgets.

DIG DEEPER

S-E-E-D VERSE:

Jeremiah 31:34

No more shall every man teach his neighbor, and every man his brother, saying, 'Know the Lord,' for they all shall know Me, from the least of them to the greatest of them, says the Lord. For I will forgive their iniquity, and their sin I will remember no more."

S – SCRIPTURE

_____

_____

_____

E – EXAMINE

_____

_____

_____

E – ENVISION

_____

_____

_____

D – DECLARE

_____

_____

_____

DAY 4

"ANCHORED"

Genesis 8:2-4 ~ The fountains of the deep and the windows of heaven were also stopped, and the rain from heaven was restrained. **3** And the waters receded continually from the earth. At the end of the hundred and fifty days the waters decreased. **4** Then the ark rested in the seventh month, the seventeenth day of the month, on the mountains of Ararat.

What a phenomenon. A historical catastrophe. A global pandemic.

There's something interesting that we should observe here. Look back at the above verses. Notice the time stamps that God took care to record in the text. *'At the end of the hundred and fifty days'* and *'in the seventh month, the seventeenth day of the month'* are both indicators of God's divine providence at work. Not only had He initiated the Flood, but He also had an exact day and time when it would stop. That's good news for us. Why? Because it proves that God's timing is flawless. He is never late or delayed. If you are walking through a flood right now, trust that in God's perfect timing, the waters will recede. The clouds will lift. The sun will shine again.

2 Peter 3:8-9 ~ But, beloved, do not forget this one thing, that with the Lord one day *is* as a thousand years, and a thousand years as one day. 9 The Lord is not slack concerning *His* promise, as some count slackness, but is longsuffering toward us, not willing that any should perish but that all should come to repentance.

God is...

- The Supreme, Invisible, Eternal Spirit-Being who existed before the physical world was formed.
- Creator of the universe, absolutely perfect in His character and nature.
- He is a Trinity - - Father, Son and Spirit.
- He is the infinite, personal God - - all-knowing, all-powerful, and everywhere present.
- He is self-existent and complete within Himself. He does not need anything or anyone to exist.
- He is self-sufficient.
- He is holy, sovereign and glorious.
- He has perfect wisdom. He is the essence of good and the exact embodiment of love.
- He is immutable - - unchangeable, timeless and timely.
- He is the first and the last, the beginning and the ending, our Everlasting King, the God Who was and is and is to come.

Let's do some digging around in 2 Peter 3:8-9.

Define the keywords in these verses:

    Forget -

    Slack -

Promise -

Longsuffering -

Perish -

Repentance -

Read the below cross reference verses:

Habakkuk 2:3

Romans 13:11

Hebrews 10:37

Galatians 4:4

What do all these verses have in common? _____

What conclusions can you draw concerning the timing of God? _____

Although the waters rose and beat violently against the Ark, it never collapsed or crumbled or sank. Instead, the waters pushed the Ark higher and higher until it found a resting place on top of the highest mountain. The same troubled waters that purged the earth of its sin and wickedness, drowning every living thing in its path, were the same waters that elevated the Ark. Why? Because God Almighty, Creator of heaven and earth, the Everlasting Father - - anchored it.

When you think of the word 'anchored,' what thoughts come to mind? _____

Anchors are nautical devices that provide security or stability to ships during harsh storms, protecting them from being tossed around at sea. Throughout history, anchors have served as a necessary tool for sailors. In the Bible, an anchor is used in a figurative sense of our hope in Jesus, Who keeps the believer secure during times of trouble or turmoil.

> Hebrews 6:19 ~ This *hope* we have as an anchor of the soul, both sure and steadfast, and which enters the *Presence* behind the veil

In the early Church, the anchor was used in artwork and engravings to symbolize Christianity as an emblem of hope. The anchor was engraved on tombstones, symbolizing the Christian's steadfast hope in eternal life.

The word *anchor* is only mentioned in the New Testament. It refers to a nautical anchor in some passages but is used metaphorically in others. Anchors are mentioned in the account of Paul's voyage to Rome during a severe storm and subsequent shipwreck (Act 27:13, 17, 29–30, 40). Jesus and His disciples are also said to have anchored their boat in Gennesaret (Mark 6:53).

When you feel overwhelmed or discouraged or weary, like the waters of life are beating against you, remember that God is your anchor.

When you feel yourself drifting away from His promises, when you are drowning in despair, when the waves of past failures, closed doors, frustrations and guilt come crashing against your shore, remember your Anchor.

Just as He anchored the Ark - - keeping it afloat, raising it up, and securing it on the mountains of Ararat - - He, too, will anchor you.

DIG DEEPER

Philippians 1:6

Being confident of this very thing, that He who has begun a good work in you will complete *it* until the day of Jesus Christ

S – SCRIPTURE

_____

_____

_____

E – EXAMINE

_____

_____

_____

E – ENVISION

_____

_____

_____

D – DECLARE

_____

_____

_____

DAY 5

"DIVINE INSTINCT"

Genesis 8:6-12 ~ 'So it came to pass, at the end of forty days, that Noah opened the window of the ark which he had made. **7** Then he sent out a raven, which kept going to and fro until the waters had dried up from the earth. **8** He also sent out from himself a dove, to see if the waters had receded from the face of the ground. **9** But the dove found no resting place for the sole of her foot, and she returned into the ark to him, for the waters *were* on the face of the whole earth. So he put out his hand and took her, and drew her into the ark to himself. **10** And he waited yet another seven days, and again he sent the dove out from the ark. **11** Then the dove came to him in the evening, and behold, a freshly plucked olive leaf *was* in her mouth; and Noah knew that the waters had receded from the earth. **12** So he waited yet another seven days and sent out the dove, which did not return again to him anymore.'

God had given Noah great details about the construction of the Ark. But He never told Noah how long he would be confined to it. How would Noah know when it was safe to leave the Ark? How would he know when the conditions were habitable? How would he know what steps, if any, to take next? Although Noah didn't have all the answers, God had given him something significant: divine instinct. It is an inner compass that leads you from a place of knowledge and truth. Divine instinct is characterized by a heart that is in perfect alignment to God, a spirit that is surrendered, and a soul (*mind, will, emotions and conscience*) that has been regenerated and sanctified. From that divine place, the Holy Spirit speaks, leads and guides. Since we know that Noah walked intimately with God and was perfect in his generation, we can be sure that his instincts came directly from God.

> 2 Peter 1:3 ~ '*as His divine power has given to us all things that pertain to life and godliness, through the knowledge of Him who called us by glory and virtue.*'

Look up the definition of instinct: _____

What do you think is the difference, if any, between gut feeling and *divine* instinct? _____

2 Corinthians 5:17 ~ Therefore, if anyone *is* in Christ, *he is* a new creation; old things have passed away; behold, all things have become new.

When the Teacher was silent during the most uncertain times, Noah didn't consult anyone else. Can you imagine the thoughts going through his mind? Surely, he could have asked his wife for direction or one of his sons (Shem, Ham, or Japheth), but we have no record that he did. Instead, Noah looked within himself for the answers.

"Greater is He that is within you than he that is in the world." - 1 John 4:4

40 days symbolizes a period of testing, trial or probation, especially before entering something new or significant. This can be seen in:

· Moses' time on Mount Sinai (Exodus 24:18, Deuteronomy 9:25)
· The spies' trip to Canaan (Numbers 13:25)
· Israel's time in the wilderness (Numbers 14:33, 32:13)
· Elijah's miraculous journey to Sinai (1 Kings 19:8)

There is another moment in Scripture where 40 days were significant.

See Matthew 4:2 and/or Luke 4:2 to find out what it is.

"To them God willed to make known what are the riches of the glory of this mystery among the Gentiles: which is Christ in you, the hope of glory." - Colossians 1:27

Using his divine instinct, at the end of forty days, Noah opened the window of the Ark and sent out a raven (Genesis 8:7). Why do you think Noah sent out a raven first?

_____

There are a few things to know about ravens. They are not picky eaters and can therefore survive on any type of food. Ravens can fly for long periods of time without rest. Ravens are also listed among the unclean birds in the Levitical Law (see Leviticus 11:13, 15). If the raven found anything dead in the waters or on the newly emerging earth, it would be satisfied. So, the raven never returned. Around that same time, Noah also sent out a dove. Often symbolized in Scripture as innocent and gentle, the dove was sent into the earth to find any signs of vegetation. Notice Noah's instinct as he waited 7 days (the number of completion and perfection) after the dove discovered an olive branch before sending it out again. But the dove did not return this time, symbolizing Noah's first offering since the Flood started.

Look back at Genesis 8:8 and make a note of how Noah sent out the dove. What are your observations when you see the words *'from himself'*? _____

Now, picture Noah holding this innocent and gentle bird in his hands. Probably praying to God that his instincts are on point. Probably whispering words of hope and faith into the atmosphere. Probably wondering when all of this will be over. And, then 'from himself,' Noah released the dove into the earth.

When the storms of life have surrounded you, it's important to remember what's in your hands. This is where innovation and creativity are at their finest. This is where divine instinct drives you to think outside the box and use what you have. Moses had a rod that he used to part the Red Sea (Exodus 14:21). David used a sling and a stone to defeat Goliath (1 Samuel 17:49). The widow used a jar of oil to launch into entrepreneurship (2 Kings 4:3-7). The disciples used borrowed fish and bread to feed thousands (Matthew 14:13-21).

What can God do with your hands, your feet, your gifts, your talents, your experiences, your intellect, your background, your anointing, your instinct?

Let's pray:
"Lord, here are my hands. Use them. In Jesus's name. Amen!"

"God was watching, but my feet were my own." - Cynthia Orivio in *"Harriet"*

DIG DEEPER

2 Timothy 2:15
Be diligent to present yourself approved to God, a worker who does not need to be ashamed, rightly dividing the word of truth.

S – SCRIPTURE

_____

_____

_____

E – EXAMINE

_____

_____

_____

E – ENVISION

_____

_____

_____

D – DECLARE

_____

_____

_____

WEEK 6

WORSHIP

DAY 1

"GO"

Genesis 8:15 - Then God spoke to Noah, saying, "Go out of the ark, you and your wife, and your sons and your sons' wives with you."

God breaks through the year-long silence and says Go.

God was essentially saying: "*There is something on the other side of the storm waiting for you. Go. Move. Act. Trust. Believe. And don't look back. As you go, the waters that once threatened you will become a memorial of My faithfulness. On the other side of the storm, there is peace like you've never imagined; revelation like you've never seen; freedom like you've always wanted; opportunity like you've never known; abundance like you've only dreamt of. Go – – because the other side is calling you.*"

"When you go through deep waters, I will be with you. When you go through rivers of difficulty, you will not drown. When you walk through the fire of oppression, you will not be burned up; the flames will not consume you." ~ Isaiah 43:2

Where is God calling you to go? _____

God's commission to 'go' meant that Noah would have to leave the very Ark that had brought him stability and protection during the storm. But in order to step toward something greater, you must be willing to leave what has been familiar to you. Like Noah, you may have to leave that which is comfortable, predictable, and secure to see the space that God has carved out specifically for you. When God says 'go', you go. Why? Because He knows what is and what is to come. (Revelation 1:8) Our trust is strengthened when we can walk into the unknown, knowing that God has already gone before us.

Where would you be willing to go if you were sure God had paved the way? _____

Write down your observations from the following verses. _____

> Deuteronomy 31:8 ~ And the Lord, He *is* the One who goes before you. He will be with you, He will not leave you nor forsake you; do not fear nor be dismayed."

> Isaiah 45:2 ~ And the Lord, He *is* the One who goes before you. He will be with you,

---

The Abrahamic Covenant is built on Abraham's willingness to leave the familiarity of his country and go to a place that God would show him. The fulfillment of this covenant extends far beyond what Abraham could see right then and into a future legacy that God Himself would secure. Read Genesis 12:1-3.

Matthew 28:19-20 ~ <u>Go</u> therefore and make disciples of all the nations, baptizing them in the name of the Father and of the Son and of the Holy Spirit, teaching them to observe all things that I have commanded you; and lo, I am with you always, *even* to the end of the age." Amen. (emphasis added)

He will not leave you nor forsake you; do
not fear nor be dismayed."

2 Samuel 5:24 ~ And it shall be, when you hear the sound of march-
ing in the tops of the mulberry trees, then you shall advance quickly.
For then the Lord will go out before you to strike the camp of the
Philistines."

Isaiah 52:12 ~ For you shall not go out with haste, nor go by flight;
For the Lord will go before you, and the God of Israel *will be* your
rear guard.

Psalm 136:16 ~ To Him who led His people through the wilderness,
for His mercy *endures* forever

Noah, along with his family, departed the Ark not knowing what conditions or circumstances they would face - - but with full confidence in a God Who had never
failed him. If God had seen Him through the worst of times, why would He abandon
Him now?

He won't. Not ever.

As we go into the final days of this study, reflect on the level of trust that God may be
calling you to. A trust that fully deserts any other alternative. A trust that is unwav-
ering. A trust that is unsinkable. A trust that cannot be extinguished or exhausted.

Where will that kind of trust take you? _____

DIG DEEPER

> **Psalm 37:5**
> Commit your way to the Lord, trust also in Him, and He shall bring *it* to pass.

S – SCRIPTURE

_____

_____

_____

E – EXAMINE

_____

_____

_____

E – ENVISION

_____

_____

_____

D – DECLARE

_____

_____

_____

DAY 2

"SEIZE THE MOMENT"

Seize the moment. This moment, right where you are. It's okay to look ahead at what's to come, but can you appreciate where you are right now?

Noah spent 120 years preaching and preparing, working and waiting.
Then God called him into the Ark of safety.
Then he spent another year in the storm of a lifetime.
Then God went silent during the test.
Then God calls him out of the Ark.
And this was Noah's response:

Genesis 8:20 - "Then Noah built an altar to the Lord..."

Perhaps Noah's mind flashed back to what the earth used to be. Or maybe he caught a glimpse of God's glory peeking through the sky. Or maybe he stood in awe of the surpassing greatness of our God. Maybe he thought about how his life, and those of his family, had been spared. Maybe he was overwhelmed by God's faithfulness. Maybe his heart was filled with so much gratitude that it literally drove him to his knees. Whatever the case, Noah didn't let the moment pass him by. His first instinct was to worship - - not to find shelter, look for food, survey the land, or anything else. Noah built an altar to the Lord!

The earth was now a blank canvas. Everything on it was new and pure. Noah responded by building an altar as his first act of worship.

What about you? What is your response when you look back on what God has done in your life? How do you seize the moment? _____

Here's a clue: build an altar and watch God meet you there.

- While you're knee-deep in your assignment, build an altar.
- While you're trying to figure out the next move, build an altar.
- While you're lost and hopeless, build an altar.
- While you're desperate for the season to pass, build an altar.
- While you're sitting for the worst test of your life, build an altar.
- While you're surrounded by flood waters, build an altar.
- While you're waiting on God to speak, build an altar.
- While you're preparing for the manifestation, build an altar.

Genesis 8:21 ~ And the LORD smelled a soothing aroma.

Noah, whether he knew it or not, had lived up to his name - - and the legacy that was declared over him at birth. When he was born, his father Lamech, *called his name Noah, saying, "This one will comfort us concerning our work and the toil of our hands, because of the ground which the LORD has cursed. (Genesis 5:29)"*

Not only did Noah bring comfort to the earth, but he was the one man who honored God in a wicked and perverse culture. He lived to tell the story of what it's like to start over. He may not have known all the details of rebuilding, replanting, or renewing. But, he knew something about worship. A soothing aroma went up to heaven and God accepted Noah's sacrifice. *And He said in His heart, "I will never again curse the ground for man's sake, although the imagination of man's heart is evil from his youth; nor will I again destroy every living thing as I have done."*

Noah took every clean animal and clean bird as a burnt offering on his altar. Since then, Jesus has been offered as the ultimate sacrifice (Hebrews 9:11-12). Now, as believers, we are to present ourselves as the *living* sacrifice.

> **Romans 12:1** ~ I beseech you therefore, brethren, by the mercies of God, that you present your bodies a living sacrifice, holy, acceptable to God, *which is* your reasonable service.

If you are a *living* sacrifice, what aroma does your life convey? _____

The only acceptable worship is you - - your life, your thoughts, your mistakes, your failures, your dreams, your goals, your expectations.

If you were to build an altar right now, what part(s) of your life would you offer to God?

_____

> Psalm 141:2 ~ Let my prayer be set before You *as* incense,
> The lifting up of my hands *as* the evening sacrifice.

May your prayers rise to the nostrils of our God like a sweet-smelling sacrifice. May you resist the urge to collapse under the pressures of this world. May your life become the perfect offering that anchors you in every season.

DIG DEEPER

Hebrews 13:15

Therefore by Him let us continually offer the sacrifice of praise to God, that is, the fruit of *our* lips, giving thanks to His name.

S – SCRIPTURE

_____

_____

_____

E – EXAMINE

_____

_____

_____

E – ENVISION

_____

_____

_____

D – DECLARE

_____

_____

_____

DAY 3

"BE FRUITFUL AND MULTIPLY"

Genesis 9:1 ~ So God blessed Noah and his sons, and said to them: "Be fruitful and multiply, and fill the earth."

The *blessing* that was initially bestowed upon Adam and Eve has been reinstated with Noah and his family. It is a reminder that God is never slack concerning His promises but is lovingly patient toward us (2 Peter 3:9). Even in His wrath, His love and mercy endures forever (Psalm 136).

It's a new beginning. A second chance. A fresh start.

	THE FIRST BEGINNING: ADAM	THE SECOND BEGINNING: NOAH
	Note the similarities between the Creation story and Noah's story.[19]	
GOD'S ACTIONS	God created Adam and Eve from the dust (2:7).	God saved Noah and his family from destruction (7:23).
GOD'S PROVISION	God planted the Garden and gave Adam and Eve plants to eat (1:29-31; 2:8).	God saved animal species along with Noah and gave Noah and his family animals for food (6:17-22).
GOD'S BLESSING	Be fruitful and multiply; have dominion over all living things (1:28).	Be fruitful and multiply; all living things will be filled with fear and dread of you (9:1, 2).
GOD'S COVENANT		Never again will God destroy the earth with a flood; He will always provide the annual seasons (8:21, 22; 9:11).
GOD'S PROHIBITION	Do not eat of the tree of the knowledge of good and evil (2:16).	Do not shed the blood of any person (9:5, 6).
GOD'S WARNING	Those who eat of it will die (2:17).	Of those who shed blood God will demand a reckoning (9:5).
GOD'S EVALUATION	It is very good (1:31).	Humanity's heart is evil (8:21).

Why do you think God never made a covenant with Adam? _____

What picture of God's grace do you see in God's blessing upon Noah and his family? _____

God's command to Noah (*be fruitful and multiply and refill the earth*) was the launching pad of a brand-new assignment. Noah had passed the test. He had not only survived the worst of days, but he was the remnant vessel that God would use to repopulate the earth. And, now the real work begins - - not only for Noah, but also for his three sons through whom all the nations, races, and languages were established (Genesis 9:19).

> **Be fruitful** - to bear fruit, be fruitful, branch off
> **Multiply** - be or become great, be or become many
> **Refill** - to fulfill, replenish, accomplish, complete

Although we're discussing fruit, it is important to note that Noah was not responsible for replanting every type of tree that we know today. The plants survived the Flood. How can we be sure of that? Look at Genesis 8:11 and note that the dove brought back a *freshly plucked olive leaf*. Growth and vegetation were happening all on their own. God never placed the burden of replanting the earth on Noah - - because the very first seeds He planted were sufficient for all eternity (Genesis 1:11-12).

Read the below verse and write down your personal observations. _____

> Psalm 52:8 ~ But I am like a green olive tree in the house of God; I trust in the mercy of God forever and ever.

When you've been faithful and obedient, you can trust that God will do the planting. Just as God planted every tree on the earth, He has planted you exactly where He wants you to be.

> The broad words *grass*, *tree* and *fruit tree* encompasses all plants, shrubs, and trees. The reference to *seed* and *kind* speaks to the fact that the plant kingdom will continue to reproduce. God not only created plant life; He also set in motion the processes that make plant life reproduce.[20] (regarding Genesis 1:11-12)

There is a purpose for you - - in that marriage, job, ministry, business, relationship, family, community. You have been planted.

Actually, say it out loud: "I have been planted."

1 Peter 1:23-25 ~ having been born again, not of corruptible seed but incorruptible, through the word of God which lives and abides forever,

> **24** because
> "All flesh *is* as grass,
> And all the glory of man as the flower of the grass.
> The grass withers,
> And its flower falls away,
>
> **25** But the word of the Lord endures forever."

Define corruptible and incorruptible from the above verse:

_____

The *incorruptible seed* that Peter refers to is the divine nature of every believer, given to us by God's divine power (2 Peter 1:4). This divine nature is implanted in seed form in the soul of believers but doesn't necessarily lead to godly, obedient living. As with any seed, our divine nature has to be cultivated (nurtured, developed, matured). The ability to *be fruitful* is already

> **Jeremiah 17:7-8** ~
> "Blessed *is* the man who trusts in the Lord, And whose hope is the Lord. For he shall be like a tree planted by the waters, Which spreads out its roots by the river, And will not fear when heat comes; But its leaf will be green, And will not be anxious in the year of drought, Nor will cease from yielding fruit.

inside you - - you just have to know it and work it. Like Noah, God would never ask you to produce something that hasn't been planted in you. As the Master Gardener,

He is well aware of what you're capable of. Give Him access to every nook and cranny of your soul - - to dig up, weed out, pluck up, and prune. When you do, you'll have no fear of storms nor drought.

Repeat this affirmation:
I have been planted by Almighty God.
I was created to produce.
The seed that He planted in me will never be destroyed, broken or unfruitful.
I am deeply rooted and will consistently bear fruit in every season.
And it is so. In Jesus's name. Amen.

If you agree that you have been planted, in what ways can you be fruitful and multiply in your everyday life? _____

_____

_____

DIG DEEPER

John 12:24
Most assuredly, I say to you, unless a grain of wheat falls into the ground and dies, it remains alone; but if it dies, it produces much grain.

S — SCRIPTURE

_____

_____

_____

E — EXAMINE

_____

_____

_____

E — ENVISION

_____

_____

_____

D — DECLARE

_____

_____

_____

DAY 4

"ANCHORED IN A NEW COVENANT"

Genesis 9:12-17 ~ And God said: "This *is* the sign of the covenant which I make between Me and you, and every living creature that *is* with you, for perpetual generations: **13** I set My rainbow in the cloud, and it shall be for the sign of the covenant between Me and the earth. **14** It shall be, when I bring a cloud over the earth, that the rainbow shall be seen in the cloud; **15** and I will remember My covenant which *is* between Me and you and every living creature of all flesh; the waters shall never again become a flood to destroy all flesh. **16** The rainbow shall be in the cloud, and I will look on it to remember the everlasting covenant between God and every living creature of all flesh that *is* on the earth." **17** And God said to Noah, "This *is* the sign of the covenant which I have established between Me and all flesh that *is* on the earth."

When you see a rainbow in the sky, what usually comes to mind? Is it a pot of gold that supposedly sits at the bottom? Or is it a reminder of God's faithfulness toward mankind?

God made a covenant with Noah (*and every living creature of all flesh),* including the animals. If an everlasting agreement can be extended to a crawling cricket, rest assured that you and your family will never be not overlooked.

One significant part of the rainbow covenant is that it didn't require anything from mankind. Covenants were generally two-party agreements - - God does this and man does that. But this covenant was God's unconditional promise, no strings attached. It is a perpetual, unbreakable covenant. Regardless of the degree of mankind's sin, God, Himself, would keep the entire covenant.

Why do you think God chose to keep the covenant Himself?

_____

_____

The entire new world would eventually be established upon God's Word, His promises and His mercy. When Noah and his sons followed out the command to '*be fruitful and multiply; fill the earth,*' they were doing so with the understanding that there

It's a wonder that Noah didn't suffer from modern-day post-traumatic stress syndrome. Can you imagine the trauma of what he witnessed? It could have lingered for the rest of his life. Perhaps to give him peace, God put a rainbow in the sky. And, now, we are beneficiaries of that same peace.

would be no more global floods. When dark clouds formed and rain poured from the sky, Noah and his descendants could look up and be reminded of God's promise.

What would you do if you had a covenant promise from God?
What could you build if you knew that God had promised to protect you?

What kind of life could you establish for yourself if you knew that God had bound Himself to you?

Isaiah 54:9-10 ~ "For this *is* like the waters of Noah to Me;
For as I have sworn
That the waters of Noah would no longer cover the earth,
So have I sworn
That I would not be angry with you, nor rebuke you.

10
For the mountains shall depart
And the hills be removed,
But My kindness shall not depart from you,
Nor shall My covenant of peace be removed,"
Says the Lord, who has mercy on you.

God made a similar covenant with Israel - - but this time referring to His kindness and peace toward them. Although the covenant refers ultimately to the millennial kingdom, believers can enjoy the promises of it today. The waters may come, but they won't drown you. The mountains and hills may disappear (as in during the Flood), but His love and peace will always be your portion.

In the book *All the Promises of the Bible*[21], author Herbert Locklear found **7,147 promises** from God to man in the Bible. With that many promises, surely you can find one that fits your current circumstances. When life seems uncertain and unfair, when you have more questions than answers, when you need reassurance, fix your gaze on what the Bible says.

Today, let's anchor ourselves to a few of those promises.

Nothing Can Separate Us from God's Love ~ Romans 8:35

All Things Will Work Out For Good ~ Romans 8:28

You Are a New Creation ~ 2 Corinthians 5:17

The Promise of Protection ~ Psalm 91:9-11

You are Healed ~ 1 Peter 2:24

God Will Be Near You ~ Psalm 145:18

Promise of Good Success ~ Joshua 1:8

There is No Condemnation ~ Romans 8:1

The Promise of Blessing ~ Deuteronomy 28:2-8

You Have Victory ~ 1 Corinthians 15:57

Our Trials Have Purpose ~ James 1:2-3

The Promise of Comfort ~ 2 Corinthians 1:3-4

The Promise of Strength ~ Isaiah 41:10

God Promises to Lead You ~ Psalm 32:8

God Will Guide You ~ Proverbs 3:5-6

Rest for Our Souls ~ Matthew 11:28-29

The Promise of Wisdom ~ James 1:5-6

God Will Order Your Steps ~ Psalm 37:23-24

God Will Lead and Teach You ~ Psalm 25:9

God's Love is For You ~ 1 John 4:16

God Promises Good Things ~ James 1:17

He Makes a Way ~ Isaiah 43:19

God Will Meet All Your Needs ~ Philippians 4:19

Jesus is Coming Soon ~ Revelation 22:20

If you could anchor yourself to any particular promise today, what would it be? __

DIG DEEPER

S-E-E-D VERSE:

2 Corinthians 1:20
For all the promises of God in Him *are* Yes, and in Him Amen, to the glory of God through us.

S – SCRIPTURE

_____

_____

_____

E – EXAMINE

_____

_____

_____

E – ENVISION

_____

_____

_____

D – DECLARE

_____

_____

_____

DAY 5

"THE NEW NORMAL"

Oh, hello! Have you noticed that a new normal has materialized? And it didn't just happen for Noah. It is evident in the events of our present day.

A new normal is defined as a state to which an economy, society, etc. settles following a crisis, when this differs from the situation that prevailed prior to the start of the crisis.[22]

Perhaps you are exactly where you should be. Perhaps this *new normal* is precisely what your soul needs. Perhaps everything that has happened up to this point has been preparing you for a new normal.

So, what now?

Where do we go from here?

For the past 6 weeks, we've been taking cues from Noah's incredible journey. In every aspect of the word, Noah was launched into an environment that was completely different - - one that he had no formal training for, one that he had no personal insight in, something new, fresh and ripe. Today, for one final time, let's see how Noah responded to his new normal.

> Genesis 9:20 ~ "And Noah began to be a farmer, and he planted a vineyard."

In his old age, Noah started a new career. He leaned into the wave of a new normal. He planted a vineyard, indicative of building a legacy that would extend far beyond himself.

Noah planted toward his destiny.

Your destiny (*the thing God created you to be and do*) predates you and will outlive you. (Ephesians 1:4)

How will you respond in this era of new normalcy?
What will you plant?
Whether it's in your family, ministry, business, community, or a body of work, plant something that will outlive you.
Build something that will stand the test of time.

> **Matthew 24:36-44** ~ "But of that day and hour no one knows, not even the angels of heaven, but My Father only.

But as the days of Noah were, so also will the coming of the Son of Man be. For as in the days before the flood, they were eating and drinking, marrying and giving in marriage, until the day that Noah entered the ark, and did not know until the flood came and took them

> Genesis 2:4-7 ~ This *is* the history of the heavens and the earth when they were created, in the day that the Lord God made the earth and the heavens, **5** before any plant of the field was in the earth and before any herb of the field had grown. For the Lord God had not caused it to rain on the earth, and *there was* no man to till the ground; **6** but a mist went up from the earth and watered the whole face of the ground.
>
> **7** And the Lord God formed man *of* the dust of the ground, and breathed into his nostrils the breath of life; and man became a living being.

all away, so also will the coming of the Son of Man be. Then two men will be in the field: one will be taken and the other left. Two women will be grinding at the mill: one will be taken and the other left. Watch therefore, for you do not know what hour your Lord is coming. But know this, that if the master of the house had known what hour the thief would come, he would have watched and not allowed his house to be broken into. Therefore you also be ready, for the Son of Man is coming at an hour you do not expect.

> Some may think the days of Noah are long past. They may think it's not that relevant. Since Noah, we've been existing under the umbrella of a new normal. And, ever so often, God does something on the earth to remind us that He is still Sovereign God.

Let's pray:

Lord, for the rest of my days, teach me to cultivate the ground until Jesus returns to establish the final and forever *new normal*. In Jesus's name. Amen!

Now, it's your turn.

Destiny is calling.

God has filled your hands with seed.

How will you respond?

DIG DEEPER

2 Corinthians 9:10
Now may He who supplies seed to the sower, and bread for food, supply and multiply the seed you have *sown* and increase the fruits of your righteousness

S – SCRIPTURE

_____

_____

_____

E – EXAMINE

_____

_____

_____

E – ENVISION

_____

_____

_____

D – DECLARE

_____

_____

_____

ENDNOTES

Week 2, Day 1:

1) Merriam-Webster. "Merriam-Webster Dictionary." *Merriam-Webster.com*, Merriam-Webster, 2022, www.merriam-webster.com/.
2) John F. MacArthur. "The MacArthur Study Bible 20th-Anniversary Edition." *Gty.org*, HarperCollins brand W Publishing, 2019, www.gty.org/store/studybible.

Week 2, Day 3:

3) Oxford University Press (OUP). "Anthropopathic." *Lexico.Com*, www.lexico.com/en/definition/anthropopathic. Accessed 3 June 2022.

Week 2, Day 5:

4) "Definition of Assignment." *www.Dictionary.Com*, www.dictionary.com/browse/assignment. Accessed 3 June 2022.
5) Murdock, Mike. *The Assignment : Powerful Secrets for Discovering Your Destiny, Dynamic Steps to Accomplish Your Life's Goals*. Albury Pub, 1997.

Week 3, Day 1:

6) Strong, James. *Strong's Exhaustive Concordance of the Bible*. Updated, Hendrickson Academic, 2009.

Week 3, Day 2:

7) "Definition of Abide." Dictionary.com. "Dictionary.com - the World's Favorite Online Dictionary!" *Dictionary.com*, Dictionary.com, 1995, www. dictionary.com/.

Week 3, Day 3:

8) "Definition of Grace." Dictionary.com. "Dictionary.com - the World's Favorite Online Dictionary!" *Dictionary.com*, Dictionary.com, 1995, www. dictionary.com/.

Week 3, Day 4:

9) Lexico. "English Dictionary, Thesaurus, & Grammar Help | Lexico.com." *Lexico Dictionaries | English*, 2019, www.lexico.com/.

10) Tenney, Merrill C. *The Zondervan Pictorial Encyclopedia of the Bible*. Regency Reference Library, 1976.

Week 3, Day 5:

11) Strong, James. *Strong's Exhaustive Concordance of the Bible*. Updated, Hendrickson Academic, 2009.

12) Brand, Chad, et al. *Holman Illustrated Bible Dictionary*. Holman Reference, 2015.

Week 4, Day 4:

13) "Definition of Refuge." Dictionary.com. "Dictionary.com - the World's Favorite Online Dictionary!" *Dictionary.com*, Dictionary.com, 1995, www. dictionary.com/.

Week 4, Day 5: The Flood Chronology

14) Hodge, Bodie. "Biblical Overview of the Flood Timeline." *Answers in Genesis*, 5 Oct. 2015, answersingenesis.org/bible-timeline/biblical-overview-of-the-flood-timeline.

Week 5, Day 1:

15) Evans, Tony, and CSB Bibles By Holman. *The Tony Evans Bible Commentary*. Holman Bible Publishers, 2019.

Week 5, Day 2:

16) "Definition of Isolation." Dictionary.com. "Dictionary.com - the World's Favorite Online Dictionary!" *Dictionary.com*, Dictionary.com, 1995, www.dictionary.com/.

17) "Footprints in the Sand." *Scrapbook.com*, https://www.scrapbook.com/poems/doc/38987.html.

Week 5, Day 3:

18) Gesenius, H., and Samuel Prideaux Tregelles. *Gesenius' Hebrew and Chaldee Lexicon to the Old Testament Scriptures: Numerically Coded to Strong's Exhaustive Concordance, with an English Index of More Than 12,000 Entries*. 7th ed., Baker Pub Group, 1979.

Week 6, Day 3:

19) Nelson, Thomas. *NKJV Study Bible, Hardcover, Burgundy, Full-Color, Comfort Print: The Complete Resource for Studying God's Word*. 3rd ed., Thomas Nelson, 2018.

20) Nelson, Thomas. *NKJV Study Bible, Hardcover, Burgundy, Full-Color, Comfort Print: The Complete Resource for Studying God's Word*. 3rd ed., Thomas Nelson, 2018.

Week 6, Day 4:

21) Lockyer, Herbert. *All the Promises of the Bible*. Revised, Zondervan Academic, 1990.

Week 6, Day 5:

22) Wikipedia contributors. "New Normal." *Wikipedia*, 18 May 2022, en.m.wikipedia.org/wiki/New_normal.

Printed in the United States
by Baker & Taylor Publisher Services